Frederick Edward Saward

The Coal Trade

A Compendium of Valuable Information

Frederick Edward Saward

The Coal Trade
A Compendium of Valuable Information

ISBN/EAN: 9783744725996

Printed in Europe, USA, Canada, Australia, Japan

Cover: Foto ©ninafisch / pixelio.de

More available books at **www.hansebooks.com**

THE COAL TRADE.

A COMPENDIUM OF VALUABLE INFORMATION

RELATIVE TO

COAL PRODUCTION, PRICES, TRANSPORTATION, ETC., AT HOME AND ABROAD, WITH MANY FACTS WORTHY OF PRESERVATION FOR FUTURE REFERENCE.

CORRECTED TO THE LATEST DATES.

BY

FREDERICK E. SAWARD,

EDITOR OF THE "COAL TRADE JOURNAL."

1876.
PUBLISHED AT 111 BROADWAY, NEW YORK.

INDEX.

	PAGE
ALBERTITE, ALBERT COAL	65
ANTHRACITE COAL production	2
" " prices	3
" " programme for 1876	6-7
ARKANSAS, coal in	60
AUSTRIA, coal resources	48
ASPHALTUM, deposits	62
BALTIMORE, MD.	29-31
BARCLAY, PA., region	8
BELVIDERE DIVISION RAILROAD, tonnage eighteen years	5
BELGIUM, coal production	49
BITUMINOUS COAL, expenses to the Atlantic seaboard	71
BITUMINOUS COAL, the districts	8
BLOSSBURG, PA., region	34
BOSTON, MASS.	9-11
BROAD TOP, region	63
BLASTING MEMORANDA	27
BUFFALO, N. Y.	24-25
CHICAGO, ILL.	31-32
CINCINNATI, OHIO	34-36
CLEVELAND, OHIO	12-14
CLEARFIELD, PA., region	67
COAL, varieties of	64
" volume of gas obtained from a ton	64
" cubic contents of a ton	66
" comparative yield of beds	67
" production of the globe	67
" first use of, as fuel	67
COAL CARS, average contents of	63
COAL PIT, deepest	73
COLORADO, coal in	19-23
CUMBERLAND, MD., region	69
COMPRESSED AIR, Properties of	4
DELAWARE & HUDSON CANAL, tonnage 45 years	4
D. L. & W. RAILROAD Co., tonnage 21 years	63
DISTANCES TO MARKET	66
DUTY ON COAL	49
FRANCE, coal production	43-44
GREAT BRITAIN	77
" working cost of collieries	
" modes of working adopted in coal mines	66
HEAT, the mechanical equivalent of	64
IMPORTS AND EXPORTS	37
ITALY, coal in	71
ILLINOIS, coal trade	61
INDIANA, coal in	74
LARGE MINE VENTILATOR	62
LAKE ERIE, coal trade on	69

	PAGE
LEHIGH NAVIGATION Co., tonnage 53 years	3
LEHIGH VALLEY RAILROAD CO., 20 years	4
MISSOURI, coal fields of	55-57
MECHANICAL STOKER	75
MOBILE, ALA.	28
MINE DRAINAGE	75
MAHOKE COUNTY, PA.	16
MCKEAN COUNTY, PA.	17
MCINTYRE, region	9
MICHIGAN, coal in	65
MORRIS CANAL, tonnage 20 years	4
MONONGAHELA, region	18
NEW SOUTH WALES, coal resources	45-47
NEW ORLEANS, LA.	33
NOVA SCOTIA	38-42
NORTHUMBERLAND COUNTY, PA., coal production	77
OHIO, coal product, etc.	57-59
PETROLEUM or coal gas light	72
PETROLEUM as fuel	75
PENNSYLVANIA COAL Co., tonnage 25 years	4
PHILA. & READING R. R. Co.	
PRUSSIA, coal trade of	50-51
PITTSBURGH, PA.	26-29
PROVIDENCE, R. I.	33
RHODE ISLAND, coal in	63
RICHMOND, VA.	31
RUSSIA, coal production	48
SPAIN, coal in	67
SNOW SHOE region	11
SOWMAN, region	14
SOMERSET COUNTY	17-18
SCHUYLKILL COAL, prices of	65
SAN FRANCISCO, CAL.	25
ST LOUIS, MO.	26
TEXAS, coal in	62
TABLE for computing prices of coal	70
TEMPERING MINING PICKS	76
UNITED STATES, coal in	71
UNDERGROUND HAULAGE of coal	63
UNDERGROUND TEMPERATURE	63
VENTILATING FURNACE	68
WEIGHT OF T RAIL	68
WEIGHT OR MEASURE	62
WEST VIRGINIA, coal resources	52-55
Gas coal region	18
WESTPHALIA	71
WESTMORELAND, region	15
WEST BRANCH, region	16
WILKESBARRE COAL & I. N Co., tonnage	5
WIRE ROPES, rules for use up in deep shafts	70
Breaking strain of	68
WESTERN KENTUCKY, coal in	76

THE COAL TRADE.

INTRODUCTION.

We present our readers with further intelligence on the important subject of coal, and ask for it a continuance of the cordial reception awarded the previous editions.

Within the year 1875, the production of Anthracite coal in America was slightly less than during the year 1874, owing to a "strike" of five month's duration—that the decrease is not larger is owing to the facilities for mining. We can now produce in six or eight months as much as was formerly produced in any given year. The Bituminous districts of Pennsylvania show a slight increase, all the other states hold about their own, although it is estimated that if we should have anything like the revival of industrial pursuits, with prosperity to the country at large, the coal product and consumption could be increased at the rate of ten per cent. per annum.

In Great Britain, and in fact in most of the foreign countries, the production has decreased, or there is but little increase, while wages and prices of coal show a marked decline. We still maintain the proud position of former years as a coal producing country, the output keeping at about fifty million tons; the Anthracite being twenty-two million tons, Bituminous and Semi-Bituminous twenty seven millions, while Colorado, Wyoming, Utah and the Pacific slope give 1,000,000 tons of *Lignite* or Brown coal annually. The Anthracite trade of the United States is profitable, as it could not fail to be, while the present organization lasts, whereby it is possible for a few companies to own or control the entire output. The Bituminous trade is fairly profitable, and the trade is being extended, taking up the increased demand that there is for fuel.

ANTHRACITE COAL.

Anthracite coal is found in an area of about 470 square miles, in Luzerne, Carbon, Schuylkill, Northumberland, Dauphin, and Columbia counties, in the State of Pennsylvania.

We append the following schedule of the production:

Year.	Tons.	Year.	Tons.
1820	365	From 1660 to 1870	114,319,161
From 1820 to 1830	533,194	1871	15,198,163
From 1830 to 1840	5,940,270	1872	18,929,263
From 1840 to 1850	21,893,153	1873	19,586,173
From 1850 to 1860	63,961,897	1874	19,785,088

There are three great divisions—which are named from their locations—the first or Southern, the second or Middle, and the third or Northern coal fields.

The Southern coal field lies principally in Schuylkill county, and hence it is often called the Schuylkill region.

The Mahanoy (often included in the Schuylkill) and Lehigh regions constitute the Middle coal field.

The Northern coal field is in Luzerne county, and embraces what is known as the Wyoming, Lackawanna, Scranton, and Wilkesbarre regions.

In addition to the production reported in our statistics it is estimated that some 3,000,000 tons are annually consumed in the coal regions by the engines, workmen, and local enterprises, the returns for which are not furnished.

The production of the three coal fields for a series of years has been as below:

Year.	Schuylkill.	Wyoming.	Lehigh.
1864	2,642,218	3,960,836	2,054,669
1865	3,735,802	3,256,638	1,922,535
1866	4,633,487	3,736,616	2,128,867
1867	4,334,620	5,328,312	2,062,446
1868	4,414,356	5,990,813	2,507,582
1869	4,748,960	6,068,365	1,929,583
1870	3,720,403	7,599,902	3,240,303
1871	5,124,760	6,481.171	2,249,356
1872	5,106,451	9,194.808	3,610,674
1873	5,209,156	10,047,241	3,243,169
1874	5,891,666	9,445,446	4,404,000

The details of the business for 1875 as also a comparison with that of the previous year is shown in the following schedule (all gross tons of 2240 pounds).

Route or Company.	Shipments to Interior Points.		Shipments to Competitive Points.		Total Shipments.	
	1875.	1874.	1875.	1874.	1875.	1874.
P. & R. R. Co.	2,999,343	3,321,890	1,785,100	2,240,759	4,784,504	5,562,649
Delaware & Hudson	1,484,141	1,974,063	1,542,117	1,456,338	3,026,258	2,430,401
Lehigh Valley R. R.	2,079,545	2,689,950	1,231,496	1,594,422	3,302,042	4,179,472
Central Railroad	1,383,648	1,584,228	1,277,986	1,388,058	2,661,635	2,972,286
D. L. & W. R. R.	1,620,515	863,554	1,318,533	1,278,978	2,939,648	2,142,533
Penn'a. Coal Co.	184,428	174,545	1,163,749	1,165,118	1,368,207	1,335,663

The range in prices during the year is shown below. We give the rates of the New York Company coals for each month, in which changes were made in the price list.

	Lump.	Steamer.	Broken.	Egg.	Stove.	Chestnut.
March	$4 60	$4 5?	$4 60	$4 75	$5 20	$4 35
April	4 60	4 70	4 60	4 95	5 40	4 40
May	4 80	4 90	5 60	5 15	5 60	4 60
June	4 90	5 00	5 10	5 25	5 70	4 70
July	5 00	5 10	5 20	5 35	5 80	4 60
August	5 00	5 10	5 20	5 45	5 90	4 90
September	5 05	5 15	5 25	5 5?	6 00	4 95
October	5 05	5 15	5 25	5 65	6 10	4 95

The rates for coals of the Philadelphia and Reading Coal and Iron Co., were based upon fifty cents per ton less than the above, f. o. b. at Philadelphia. The price lists for January and February were nominally those of December 1874—for N. Y. Co.'s Lump $5.55; Steamer $5.65; Broken $5.75; Egg $5.90; Stove $6.40; Chestnut $5.35. For November and December 1875, rates were nominally as per October price list.

The rate of transportation charged by Reading Railroad Company on the individual coal carried during the early part of the year 1875, was $1.67 per ton, advancing to $1.92 before the close, subject to drawbacks on coal sold on contract; the rate from Mauch Chunk by rail to the tide-water shipping ports was $2.41 per ton in the early part of the year, and $2.10 at the close; as the suspension was general for the first half of the year, the latter rate may be said to be the expense on coal, free of shipping charges.

Coastwise freights during the year were low from all points, and this enabled considerably more tonnage to be moved, than would otherwise have been the case.

As showing the value of Anthracite for metallurgical purposes, we append the following results of analyses made for that purpose by J. B. Britton, Esq., of Philadelphia.

	Wyoming.	Schuylkill.	Lehigh.
Moisture	1.38	1.35	1.20
Vol. Combustible Matter	3.52	3.78	3.05
Ash	3.24	5.61	3.54
Fixed Carbon	91.56	89.06	92.11
	100.00	100.00	100.00

ANTHRACITE COAL TONNAGES.

The Lehigh Coal and Navigation Company began the mining and shipment of coal in 1820 with 365 tons; in 1874 the mining portion of the Company's business was merged into the Lehigh and Wilkesbarre Coal Co.—Statistics showing the progress of business are as below:

Years.	Tons.	Years.	Tons.	Years.	Tons.
1820	365	1845	257,740	1870	408,979
1825	28,390	1850	494,156	1871	762,073
1830	48,000	1855	449,819	1872	1,014,400
1835	131,250	1860	517,157	1873	1,041,153
1840	102,244	1865	517,025		

THE COAL TRADE.

The **Morris Canal** began carrying coal in the year 1845. Statistics showing the progress of business are as below:

Years.	Tons.	Years.	Tons
1845	12,567	1870	309,843
1850	90,100	1871	315,610
1855	290,730	1872	341,963
1860	404,464	1873	301,214
1865	416,189	1874	267,605

The **Delaware and Hudson Canal Company** began the mining and carrying of coal in the year 1829; the progress of their business is shown below:

Years.	Tons.	Years.	Tons.
1829	7,000	1871	1,308,471
1830 to 1839	846,330	1872	2,930,761
1840 to 1849	2,897,981	1873	2,752,595
1850 to 1859	4,638,655	1874	2,399,417
1860 to 1869	10,099,691	1875	3,066,479
1870	2,039,792		

The **Philadelphia and Reading Railroad Company** began the carrying of coal in the year 1850; business has been increased as below:

Years.	Tons.	Years.	Tons.
1850	1,351,502	1871	6,002,573
1855	2,213,292	1872	6,185,434
1860	1,946,195	1873	6,546,553
1865	3,090,814	1874	6,349,812
1870	4,633,504	1875	5,505,454

The **Delaware, Lackawanna and Western Railroad** began in the year 1854, the business has been as below:

Years.	Tons.	Years.	Tons.
1854—59	2,629,364	1872	2,836,943
1860—69	13,343,126	1873	3,136,306
1870	2,248,097	1874	2,570,437
1871	1,916,486	1875	3,326,901

The **Pennsylvania Coal Co.**, commenced business in the year 1850; their product has been as follows:

Years.	Tons.	Years.	Tons
1850—59	4,834,723	1872	1,213,478
1860—69	7,249,820	1873	1,239,214
1870	1,086,008	1874	1,398,663
1871	802,069	1875	1,364,207

The **Lehigh Valley Railroad Company** began the carrying of coal in the year 1855; the progress of their business is shown below;

Years.	Tons.	Years.	Tons.
1855	8,492	1872	3,850,119
1860	730,641	1873	4,144,339
1865	1,687,462	1874	4,150,659
1870	3,603,556	1875	3,277,571
1871	2,889,074		

THE COAL TRADE.

THE BELVIDERE DIVISION of Pennsylvania Railroad was opened for traffic in the year 1857; the business has progressed as follows:

Years.	Tons.	Years.	Tons.
1857	120,946	1871	682,407
1860	146,306	1872	945,808
1865	214,945	1873	1,155,209
1870	714,217	1874	1,227,966
1875			1,227,19

THE WILKESBARRE COAL AND IRON Co., began mining in 1869; merged into LEHIGH AND WILKESBARRE COAL Co., in 1874. The business is shown below:

Years.	Tons	Years.	Tons.
1869	542,455	1873	1,178,407
1870	799,296	1874	2,479,392
1871	960,754	1875	2,995,098
1872	1,148,716		

THE COAL TRADE.

THE PROGRAMME FOR 1876.

We are enabled to lay before our readers a statement of the prices of coal and basis of operations for 1876, as fixed upon by the combined Anthracite coal producing companies. A meeting of the parties in interest held during February, organized as the Board of Control, electing Mr. Thomas Dickson, President of the Delaware and Hudson Canal Co., as President, and Franklin B. Gowen, of the Philadelphia and Reading Railroad, and Philadelphia and Reading Coal and Iron Co., as Secretary. The rules adopted by the Board of Control are as below:

We, the undersigned committee, submit the following plan for the government of the anthracite coal trade to competitive points for the year 1876, viz:

I. Competitive tonnage shall embrace all coal which, for final consumption or in transitu, reaches any point upon the Hudson river or the Bay of New York, or which passes out of the Capes of the Delaware, including all sizes except pea coal: provided that nothing shall be accounted as pea coal which will not pass through a screen-mesh of three-quarters of an inch square.

II. For the purpose of making a pro rata distribution, the competitive tonnage for the year 1876—i. e., from January 1 to December 31—shall be assumed to be eight millions five hundred thousand tons, which amount shall be divided among the several parties hereto as follows:

	Per cent.	Tons.
Reading Railroad	25.57	2,173,450
Delaware and Hudson Canal	18.18	1,545,800
Central Railroad of New Jersey	15.98	1,358,300
Lehigh Valley Railroad	15.80	1,343,000
Delaware, Lackawana and Western	13.65	1,160,250
Pennsylvania Coal Company	10.82	919,700
		8,500,000

III. That the aggregate tonnage awarded to each interest, as above, shall, prior to February 20, be divided into monthly shipments for the entire season, including in such division the actual shipments for the period of the year already elapsed, and when such division is made and approved by the Board of Control it shall represent the monthly quota of each interest for each month respectively. If during any month the aggregate shipments to competitive points exceed or are less than the aggregate of all the monthly quotas for such month, the excess or deficiency, as the case may be, shall be distributed to or be borne by the several interests in the proportion of their respective yearly quotas, the object being that any excess or diminution of tonnage over or under the assumed amount of eight million five hundred thousand tons shall be divided according to the yearly quotas, and not according to the monthly quotas of the months in which such excess or diminution occurs, so that at the end of the year the entire competitive tonnage shall be divided amongst all the interests in the exact proportion of their respective yearly quotas.

IV. That on or before the tenth day of each month each interest shall make a return to the secretary of the Board of Control of the entire coal production and shipments of its region or district, giving the origin of all coal tonnage, with such detail of the destination and distribution thereof into local and competitive, as may be required by the secretary, in order to enable him to examine into and vouch the correctness of the several items; and in addition thereto, the shipping books and tonnage accounts of each company shall at all times be open to the inspection and examination of any member of the association or of his authorized agent.

V. That at the meeting of the Board of Control held next preceding the twentieth of each month the secretary shall make return showing the actual shipments of each interest for the preceding month, together with the excess or deficiency of each, calculated as hereinabove provided; and thereupon each interest which is in excess of its proper shipment shall pay to the secretary and treasurer the sum of one dollar and fifty cents for each ton of such excess, for distribution by the said secretary and treasurer, at the rate of one dollar and fifty cents per ton, amongst those who have fallen short of the amount due to them in said month.

VI. That a committee of six, consisting of one representative from each interest, to be named by such interest, be appointed as a Board of Control for the year, who shall elect one of their members as president and another as secretary and treasurer, and who shall meet at least once a month, and as much oftener as they may determine to be necessary, and who shall have power—

(a.) To establish from time to time the monthly prices at which coal shall be sold.

(b.) To provide for the increase or curtailment of the total quantity to be shipped to competitive points in any month, according to the requirements of the market.

(c.) To provide for the collection from time to time from all the members, in the proportion of their yearly quotas, any funds which may be necessary to pay the expenses incurred or authorized by the Board of Control.

(d.) To employ the services of an expert accountant, as an assistant to the secretary and treasurer, to keep the tonnage accounts of the several companies, and to receive, examine and report upon the tonnage returns received from each interest.

VII. That in establishing prices for coals the white ash coal of the different regions shall be the basis, and for such coals the price free on board in New York shall be thirty-five cents per ton above the free on board price in Philadelphia for all sizes except chestnut coal, which, at the option of the Philadelphia and Reading Coal and Iron Company, may be seventy cents per ton less in Philadelphia than in New York; Provided, that any interest may adopt higher prices for all or any of its coals than those established by the Board of Control; but Lehigh lump coal shall be fifty cents higher than other white ash lump coal.

VIII. That no commission shall be allowed on any sales of coal, and in lieu thereof, there shall be a contractors' circular price established for each month, for all such yearly contractors as shall, prior to April 1, make application, which shall be accepted for a fixed amount of coal to be taken during the year in regular monthly instalments, which price shall be twenty cents per ton less than the general circular rate at which transient orders are taken. The form of such contracts to be approved by the Board of Control.

IX. The contractors' prices for the month of March be as follows, free on board in New York:

Lump.................$4 40 Egg...................$4 70
Steamer...............4 50 Stove.................5 30
Grate.................4 60 Chestnut..............4 30

X. That season contracts with consumers only be made for lump, steamer broken and chestnut coals, at the following rates, viz., free on board at New York:

	Lump.	Steamer.	Broken.	Chestnut.
March and April	$4 20	$4 30	$4 40	$4 40
May	4 26	4 35	4 45	4 40
June	4 30	4 40	4 50	4 40
July	4 35	4 45	4 55	4 45
August	4 40	4 50	4 60	4 50
September	4 45	4 55	4 65	4 55
October	4 50	4 60	4 70	4 60
November	4 55	4 65	4 75	4 65
December	4 60	4 70	4 80	4 70

and at thirty-five cents per ton less free on board in Philadelphia, except for chestnut coal, which may be seventy cents per ton less than the free on board price in New York. It being provided that all such contracts shall be made in writing prior to April 1, and that no commissions or allowances of any kind be made thereon, and that no such contracts be made with any other than a consumer of coal.

XI. That all sales to be made for cash, or with seven per cent. interest added in all cases for any deferred payment, the interest to commence from the date of the bill of lading, and all deliveries of coal be charged at the circular prices current in the month when the delivery is made, and under no circumstances shall any coal shipped in one month be charged at the circular prices of a preceding month, unless the purchaser had a vessel at the shipping point ready to receive the coal before the expiration of the previous month, and was actually entitled to receive the coal during such previous month.

XII. That no coal shall be sold by any party in any other manner than is above provided, or at any less prices, either directly or indirectly, than those above named, or which may from time to time be established as the monthly circular rates by the Board of Control.

XIII. That nothing but competitive tonnage shall be subject to the direction of the Board of Control, and that each interest shall have the absolute and exclusive control of its local trade.

XIV. That each transporting company shall be held responsible for the faithful adherence to these regulations on the part of all individual shippers using its lines to carry coal to competitive points.

Respectfully submitted.

THOMAS DICKSON, } Committee.
FRANKLIN B. GOWEN, }

New York, February 18, 1873.

THE BITUMINOUS COAL DISTRICTS.

PENNSYLVANIA.

BLOSSBURG REGION.

The first coal from this region was sent to market from the Bloss mines in 1840. The producers of this region are the Fall Brook Coal Company, Morris Run Coal Company, and Blossburg Coal Company, with mines near Blossburg, Tioga county, Pa.

Seventy-five miles of railway, carries the coal from the Blossburg region to Seneca lake, in New York State, where it is received into canal boats which deliver it throughout the State. The railway from the mines connects with the Erie Railway at Corning. N. Y., affording additional outlet for the coal from this region.

The most important seam is that known as the Bloss vein, a clean bed of pure coal, from 4½ to 5½ feet in thickness.

Statistics of the output are shown in the following schedule.

Year.	Tons.	Year.	Tons.
1840	4,235	1871	815,079
1850	23,161	1872	849,262
1860	78,918	1873	991,057
1865	394,642	1874	796,888
1870	733,035	1875	581,782

BARCLAY REGION.

This region is located in Bradford county, Pa., some 36 miles south from Waverly, N. Y. The mines are owned by the Fall Creek Bituminous Coal Co., and the Erie Railway Co., (comprising the lands formerly of the Barclay, the Towanda Coal Co. and the Schrader Coal Co.'s).

The following table shows the amount of coal shipped from the Barclay, Coal Region, by the several companies which have operated it :

Year	Barclay Coal Co.	Towanda Coal Co.	Fall Creek Coal Co.	Total Products.
1856	2,295	....	....	2,295
1857	6,265	....	....	6,265
1858	17,560	....	....	17,560
1859	30,143	....	....	30,143
1860	27,718	....	....	27,718
1861	40,835	....	....	40,835
1862	52,779	....	....	52,779
1863	54,535	....	....	54,535
1864	62,058	....	....	62,058
1865	49,375	7,886	10,936	73,197
1866	37,963	31,681	29,004	99,453
1867	30,119	27,668	16,953	74,739
1868	....	67,080	6,595	73,675
1869	....	176,307	4,303	180,610
1870	————	196,310	77,025	273,335
1871	Schrader	249,240	129,095	378,335
1872	Coal Co.	263,960	118,882	382,842
1873	....	252,329	85,315	337,644
1874	100,219	215,572	21,281	337,072
1875	157,656	200,424	18,557	376,637

MCINTYRE REGION.

The McIntyre Coal Co., whose mines are at Ralston, Pa., on the Northern Central Railway (54 miles from Elmira, N. Y.), which gives them an outlet both north and south to a market, commenced operations in 1870.

Statistics of their business are as below:

Year	Tons.	Year	Tons.
1870	17,802	1873	212,468
1871	106,186	1874	139,907
1872	111,490	1875	164,367

Since the opening of the mines of the Blossburg district in 1840 the shipments by each company have been as follows:

Arbon Coal Company 1840—1843	40,683 net tons.
Wm. M. Mallory, 1844—1857	406,113 "
D. S. Magee, 1856—1859	78,996 "
Tioga Transportation Company	373,174 "
Salt Company of Onondaga, 1853—1866	247,809 "
Morris Run Coal Company, 1864—1875	3,340,057 "
	—3,981,670 "
Fall Brook Coal Company, 1860—1875	2,946,793 "
Blossburg Coal Company, 1866—1875	1,604,344 "
Total production of the District	9,066,517 "

BROAD TOP REGION.

The area of this coal field is stated at 80 square miles, and the aggregate thickness of workable coal seams is 26 feet, the larger seams range from five to ten feet in thickness, and the lesser from one to three.

An outlet for the coal from this region is afforded by the Huntingdon and Broad Top Mountain Railroad (this was completed in 1856, and during the latter part of that year, 42,000 tons were forwarded from this region to various markets). This line extends from the town of Huntingdon, on the Pennsylvania Railroad, 203 miles west of Philadelphia, to Mt. Dallas in Bedford county, a distance of 45 miles. At Saxton, 24 miles from Huntingdon, a branch road, 10 miles in length, extends to Broad Top City; at Riddlesburg, 5 miles beyond Saxton, is another branch in to Fulton, 5 miles from the main road.

From Mt. Dallas the Bedford and Bridgeport Railroad, 38 6-10 miles in length, extends to the Maryland State line; from this point to Cumberland, Md., via the C. and P. R. R., is 7 miles. This connection gives an outlet to the George's Creek Cumberland coal to the interior markets of Pennsylvania, to Philadelphia and South Amboy, N. J. The Bedford and Bridgeport road is leased to the Pennsylvania Railroad and operated by them.

The yearly shipments from this region, by the H. & B. T. R. R., have been as follows:

Year	Tons.	Year	Tons.
1856	42,000	1866	263,790
1857	78,613	1867	244,413
1858	106,478	1868	290,984
1859	130,506	1869	360,778
1860	154,208	1870	313,495
1861	272,625	1871	319,696
1862	338,644	1872	197,473
1863	295,678	1873	350,945
1864	346,645	1874	226,698
1865	315,905	1875	304,291

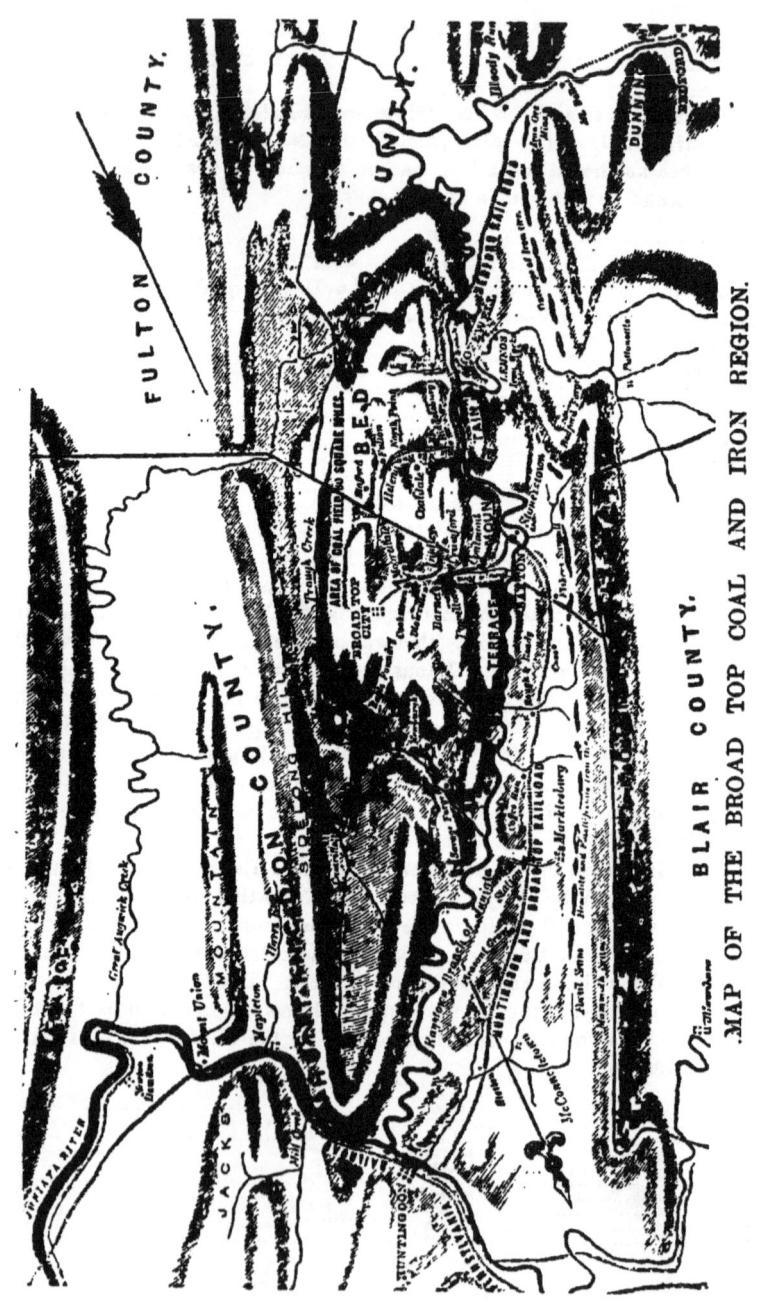

MAP OF THE BROAD TOP COAL AND IRON REGION.

The East Broad Top Railroad, penetrated this coal field during 1875, and carried 53,567 tons of coal in that year.

The shipments of Cumberland coal over the Pennsylvania State line, and H. & B. T. R. R., have been as below:

1872.........................82,021 tons.   1874.........................67,671 tons.
1873.........................114,569 "   1875.........................175,134 "

In regard to the prices obtained for this coal, we are informed that the following are the average rates, f. o. b. at Philadelphia:

Years	Price.	Years	Price.
1863	$5.75	1869	$4.75
1864	6.50	1870	4.50
1865	7.25	1871	4.60
1866	6.75	1872	4.70
1867	4.75	1873	5.00
1868	4.50	1874	4.55
		1875	$4.15

The details of the business for 1875, and names of operators are as below:

Colliery.	Operator.	Tons sent to market in 1875.
Cumberland,	R. Langdon & Co.,	14,672
Crawford.	do.	
Powelton,	R. H. Powel & Co.,	23,926¼
Barnet,	R. U. Jacob & Co.,	8,421½
Dudley,	J. M. Bacon,	2,640½
Blair,	do.	2,395¾
Howe,	do.	8,989
Mooredale,	Reakirt Bros. & Co.,	20,904
Fisher,	Fishers & Miller,	15,292½
Carbon,	Geo. Mears,	20,351
Mount Equity,	Kemble C. & I. Co.,	41,738¼
Cunard,	R. B. Wigton,	19,717
Scott,	William Scott,	212¼
Helena,	E. P. Jenkins,	539¾
Coaldale,	Wm. H. Piper,	24,737½
Rommell,	Maher & Wilson,	383¼
Total for 1875.		204,920¾

SNOW SHOE REGION.

This region is located in Centre county, Pennsylvania, covers an area of about eight miles in length, and some four miles in breadth, and is situated on both sides of Beach Creek. The coal finds an outlet to market, via the Bellefonte and Snowshoe and Bald Eagle Valley connections of the Pennsylvania Railroad, it being 47 miles from Snowshoe to Tyrone on the main line.

There is but one company mining in this district. It commenced opera-

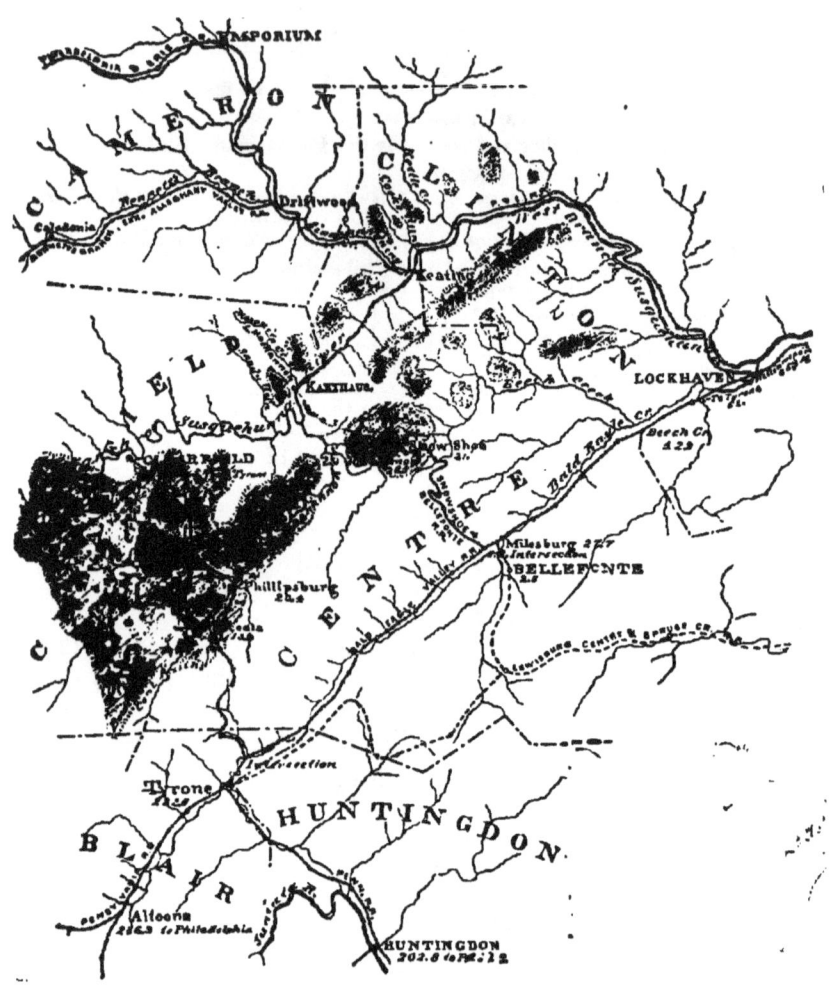

MAP OF THE CLEARFIELD. REGION

THE COAL TRADE.

tions in the year 1862, with 8,260 tons, and has increased as below:

Years	Tons	Years	Tons
1902	8,260	1869	49,265
1903	12,699	1870	95,274
1864	26,599	1871	79,944
1865	51,831	1872	69,991
1866	70,990	1873	96,967
1867	68,137	1874	63,540
1868	60,149	1875	62,486

Prof. Rogers gives this Snowshoe coal 78.8 of Fixed Carbon, and 21.2 of Volatile Matter and Ashes.

CLEARFIELD REGION.

The district known as the "Clearfield," is located in Clearfield and Centre counties, in the State of Pennsylvania.

It has within a few years become a most important producer of Semi-Bituminous coal, and has made a market in the interior cities and towns of Pennsylvania and New Jersey, at Philadelphia, Baltimore, New York and the Eastern States.

The coal measures are found to be admirably adapted for working, dipping gently toward the Moshannon Creek, which flows through the centre of the basin. The lowest seam of coal (A), five feet thick, crops out on the level of this stream. The next (B), sixty feet above, is three to four feet in thickness. Fifty feet above is another seam (C), ranging from two to three and a half feet in thickness. Again, fifty feet above, is found a seam (D) of five feet of good solid coal.

The coal is used for steam purposes under stationary, marine, or locomotive engines, for making iron and steel rails, for glass works, in lime kilns, and for many other purposes, being much liked wherever used; ignites freely, burns readily, and leaves a white ash. It is not easily friable, and bears transportation remarkably well.

The outlet for the coal from this region is by connections with the Tyrone and Clearfield Branch of the Pennsylvania Railroad, extending from Tyrone on the main line, (224 miles west from Philadelphia), to Clearfield, 41 miles. Another, via Karthaus and Keating is projected which will shorten the distance to Philadelphia, and the grades will be more favorable.

The Pennsylvania Railroad Company own the railroads, the shipping wharves, and all the means of access to the markets of the Atlantic seaboard; the advantage of being connected with a railroad of such magnitude, and wonderful ramifications and communications, gives the coal proprietors of this region great facilities for the proper conduct of their buisness.

Mining operations began in this region in 1862; from that date to 1870 we are informed that there has been forwarded 696,377 tons.

THE COAL TRADE.

Years	Tons.	Years	Tons.
In 1870	410,523	In 1873	592,860
In 1871	542,896	In 1874	639,630
In 1872	431,915	In 1875	915,673

Analyses of coal from this district made by the State Geological Survey of 1875, gave:

	Name of Colliery	Water.	Volatile matter.	Fixed carbon.	Sulphur.	Ash.
	Clearfield County.					
1.	Penn Colliery	.810	20.640	74.023	.507	4.020
2.	Franklin Colliery	.670	21.360	74.284	.435	3.251
3.	Eureka Mine	.780	21.680	73.052	.688	3.800
4.	Stirling Mine	.710	23.400	72.218	.532	3.140
5.	Moshannon Colliery	.765	20.090	74.779	.666	3.700
6.	New Moshannon Mine	1.100	23.070	71.199	.611	4.020
7.	Hale's Colliery. Upper bed	.570	24.630	68.400	1,900	4.500
8.	Hale's Colliery. Lower bed	.740	25.210	68.628	2.122	3 300
9.	Mapleton Colliery	.700	23.565	68.890	1.715	5.130
10.	Logan Colliery	.620	22.135	68.726	.867	7.650
11.	Laurel Run Colliery	.800	23.260	72.350	.190	3.000
12.	Decatur Coal Co.'s Colliery. Lower bench	.640	24.360	64.082	3.378	7.540
13.	Decatur Coal Co.'s Colliery. Upper bench	.820	23.900	69.007	1.373	4.900
14.	Morrisdale Mine. Lower bench	.550	24.090	71.689	.571	3.100
15.	Morrisdale Mine. Upper bench	.560	25.190	71.013	.587	2.650
16.	Derby Colliery	.410	22.810	66.690	1.790	8.300
17.	Reitur's Colliery. Upper bed	.630	24.630	70.896	.654	3.690
18.	Mon's Mine	.750	19.570	69.833	.677	9.170
19.	Hill's Mine	.380	22.250	67.995	2,455	6.890
20.	Humphrey's Mine	.410	21.800	72.903	1.097	3.800
21.	Mason's Mine. Upper bench	.550	22.650	72.616	1.334	2.650
22.	Mason's Mine. Lower bench	.480	22.320	59.788	4.232	13.180
23.	G. W. Davis' Mine	.640	23.010	71.799	.551	4.000
24.	Jeremiah Cooper's Mine	.700	24.020	64.951	1,639	8.690
25.	Williamson's Mine	.620	22.730	68.784	1.576	6.280
26.	Powelton Mine. Lower part of bed	.600	22.600	68.709	2.691	5.400
27.	Powelton Mine. Upper part of bed	.640	22.560	71.551	1,079	4.270
28.	Webster's Colliery	1.630	22.000	72.815	.425	3.130
29.	Bell's Mine	.950	32.450	59.904	1.296	5.400
30.	Tyler's Mine	.940	31.060	61.563	1.487	4.950
31.	R. Shaw's Mine	.870	21.680	68.928	1.302	7.220
32.	J. Shaw's Mine	.520	21.030	67.183	.767	10.550
33.	Mongold's Mine	.860	31.600	61.602	2.228	3,590
34.	Hubler's Mine	.420	25.010	67.221	2,479	4.870
35.	Beaver Run	.920	21.550	74.009	.631	2.890
	Centre County.					
1.	Snow Shoe Mines. Upper bed. Mine No. 5	1.280	25.560	68.937	.613	3.590
2.	Snow Shoe Mines. Middle bed. Mine No. 6	.650	24.560	70.416	.964	3.410
3.	Snow Shoe Mines. Lower bed (B). Mine No. 4	.750	23.440	64.374	.986	10.450
4.	Wm. Holt's Mine, west of Holt's Hill	.880	28.620	70.089	.681	4.750
5.	Wm. Holt's Mine, Snow Shoe basin. Upper b'h	1.680	21.870	71.108	.612	4.730

SONMAN.

This district lies in Cambria county, the coal worked is the same vein that is mined in Clearfield county; the coal here has a heavier cover than where found in the adjoining county of Clearfield, is strong, and partakes somewhat of the nature of the gas coal found in Westmoreland county, which adjoins it on the south west; the trade has largely increased during the two years past, shipments having been made to all tide water ports, to New England, Baltimore, Chicago, Cleveland, etc., at the west, and along the line of the Pennsylvania Railroad, it has not only maintained its place, but gained in favor.

Analysis made of the Sonman coal from this district gave the following results as compared with Broad Top and Westmoreland.

THE COAL TRADE.

	I.	II.	Broad Top.	West-moreland.
Volatile matter	18.80	17.70	17.85	32.55
Fixed Carbon	78.60	79.20	74.65	61.45
Ash	2.70	2.70	7.50	5.80
Sulphur	0.40	0.40	1.86	1.04

No. I. was made by Dr. Charles M. Cresson, and II. by Messrs. Booth & Garrett; the yield of coke showed 82.30 per cent.; taking Pennsylvania coal as the standard for steam, the Sonman is equivalent to .959.

MONONGAHELA REGION.

This district may truly be called the perfection of a coal region. The Monongahela river for 95 miles, possesses every advantage for facilitating the production of coal, and it is not surprising that the tonnage is so immense. The seam worked is of uniform thickness, and yields a pure coal, used for iron making, steam raising, and for gas and domestic purposes.

By means of its slack-water navigation, the Monongahela river is made navigable at all seasons of the year, and boats carrying 800 tons are passed down. The city of Pittsburgh is supplied mainly by railroad, and the larger portion of the coal going down by the river, is run down the Ohio and Mississippi to the lower markets. The boats in use are known as "broad horns" carrying 20,000 bushels, "barges" carrying 11,000 bushels, and "flats" carrying 2,000 bushels. The following statement of shipments by the slack-water navigation, from 1845 to date, is of interest:

Year	Tons.	Year	Tons.
1845	184,900	1860	1,517,909
1846	311,156	1861	834,620
1847	888,805	1862	743,358
1848	392,774	1863	1,131,150
1849	296,340	1864	1,402,998
1850	491,918	1865	1,550,791
1851	490,850	1866	1,704,212
1852	655,238	1867	1,902,908
1853	628,654	1868	1,812,040
1854	696,278	1869	2,100,504
1855	869,360	1870	2,308,566
1856	853,364	1871	1,944,582
1857	1,156,969	1872	2,291,280
1858	1,027,666	1873	2,094,312
1859	1,131,467	1874	2,518,504
	1875	2,275,265	

WESTMORELAND GAS COAL.

This well known coal is mined near Penn and Irwin stations, on the Pennsylvania Railroad, in Westmoreland county; the distance from Philadelphia is 332 miles. The coal mined is the great Pittsburgh bed of bituminous coal; the companies operating in this region are large and influential, doing a business of about a million tons annually; the coal is used in every seaboard city for gas purposes, and commands a high price. The shipping points are South Amboy, N. J., and Greenwich on the Delaware river. The product for 1874 was 952,971 tons, and for 1875, 769,968 tons, (including 36,273 tons coke), the decrease was owing to a long and vexatious strike in the early part of the year.

This coal is in great favor among gas engineers in the United States.

In the dry way, by the ordinary process, the Westmoreland coal yields on an average sample as follows :

Charge, 224 pounds, carbonized 3 h. 20 m., produced per ton..................9,500 cu. ft.
Illuminating power, standard Argand...16,62 candles.
Weight of coke, per ton...1,544 pounds.
Bushels of coke, per ton...40
Maximum yield of gas per ton...10,642 cu. ft.
One bushel of lime purified..6,420 cu. ft.

Analysis of the coal :

Volatile matter..36 per cent.
Fixed carbon..58 "
Ash..6 "
                                                              100

Value of the gas from one ton estimated in pounds of spermacetti ....541.26 pounds

The above results were obtained in the experimental works of the Manhattan Gas Light Company, New York, where the daily average yield of gas from this coal and its equivalent, the "Penn," is about 10,000 cubic feet of seventeen candle gas.

MERCER COUNTY, PENNSYLVANIA.

The most important coal region in North-west Pennsylvania (running over into Eastern Ohio), is that of Mercer county. The coal produced is what is known as the splint or block coal, and is used in the raw state for smelting iron ; the principal location of this peculiar coal is on the Erie and Pittsburgh Railroad, about 75 miles south from Erie, and finds an outlet to market by this route and the Beaver and Erie canal. The beds vary from two to five feet in thickness, and some half million tons are annually produced, the figures for 1873 aggregating 529,496 net tons.

WEST BRANCH REGION.

The Philadelphia and Erie Railroad runs across the northern ends of five coal basins. There is no important development of the first two. In the third, at 67 miles west of Williamsport, is the Wistar Mountain Co.'s mines; at 97 miles, are the works of the Cameron Coal Co. In the fourth, at 117 miles, is St. Mary's; at 125 miles, Benzinger's; at 128 miles, the Shawmut branch road comes in. In the fifth, at 138 miles, are the Johnsonburg mines. The completion of the Philadelphia, New York and Buffalo Railroad gives the coal from these basins an outlet to an additional market ; 81,742 net tons were shipped in 1873, and 162,000 tons in 1874.

McKEAN COUNTY, PENNSYLVANIA.

The body of coal in the fifth basin, in the southern part of McKean county, is so large and important, and is situated so near the Buffalo and Rochester markets, that the district is entitled to more than ordinary notice. In Sargeant township, at Bishop's Summit, on the head-waters of the Instanter, running into the Clarion on the South, and on Red Mill brook, running into Potato creek and the Allegheny river on the north-east, is a large solid body of several thousand acres of unbroken coal measures. No other coal basin contains so large a body of coal at its northern extremity as this, owing probably to its being situated on the dividing waters where the work of denudation has been less destructive. An excellent railroad route renders the region accessible by a branch from the Buffalo, New York and Philadelphia Railroad at Larrabee's up the valley of Potato creek, past Smethport, and by Red Mill brook to Bishop's Summit, the distance being but 108 miles to Buffalo, and 150 to Rochester.

Analyses and practical tests of considerable quantities of this coal, under stationary and locomotive boilers, indicate that it is a good quality of bituminous coal for gas, with excellent steam-generating qualities. No other county in Northern Pennsylvania, not even Tioga, contains so much coal as McKean. A large company, composed of Buffalo capitalists and others, called "The Buffalo Coal Company," has been organized for the development of this region, and are now vigorously engaged in mining and shipping. During 1875, while at work only six months, the business was 131,190 tons. We give the following analyses of three samples, from the State survey report for 1875.

Water	1.130	1.300	1.170
Volatile matter	33.090	39.830	36.440
Fixed carbon	58.006	52.069	43.992
Sulphur	1.874	1.727	1.708
Ash	10.900	5.080	17.620

SOMERSET COUNTY, PENN'A.

In Somerset county, Pennsylvania, and adjoining the Cumberland region of Maryland is the coal field known as the Myer's mills or Salisbury region, said to be an extension of the Cumberland coal basin. The coal is of the same quality and will yield an equal quantity per acre. It is eleven miles from Frostburg, Md., (on the line of the Pittsburgh, Washington and Baltimore Railroad.) and the coal finds an outlet to Baltimore, etc., over this line and the main stem of the B. & O. R. R. The Keystone Coal Co. have been at work here since 1872, and have already built up an established business ranging from 250 to 600 tons per day according to the season : the property of the company is advantageously situated for the shipment of its production, and the rate of transportation from the mines to market is very favorable. The Cumberland and Elk Lick Coal Co. own 1,500 acres of land in this disirict, and have been doing a small business, putting the mines in order for a larger trade in the near future.

Myers mills, which may be stated as the centre of the district, is 217 miles from Baltimore, and 112 miles from Pittsburgh, by present routes

The first coal seam rests on a thin floor of fire clay. The coal bed has two benches; the lower, 18 inches thick, is an impure cannel coal circling to block structure; the upper is a medium quality of semi-bituminous coal with the well marked columnar structure peculiar to Allegheny coals.

The interval between this and the next small coal seam is composed of thin plates of sandstones with olive-colored shales.

The second workable seam (B) is pre-eminently *the bed* of the lower system of coal measures; not, perhaps, so much from its size and good quality of coal, as from its ready and sure identification, wherever it exists, by the massive bed of limestone on which it rests. The farmers trace it from hillside to hillside, regarding it with peculiar affection as a *double gift*—not only supplying fuel for domestic use, but also with lime to enrich the "glades" in their mountain farms.

The coal in this bed is columnar in structure with plates of mineral charcoal disseminated. In structure and quality it is closely associated with the best Clearfield coal. It will be found a superior fuel for iron working.

The third seam (C) is all pure coal of an excellent quality; but as the bed is high in the measures and does not occupy a wide area in this portion of the field, it has as yet received little attention.

From seam (B) to the top of the scale the measures are composed of very soft flesh and olive colored shales, which have been rounded and softened into easy rolling slopes and rounded hills.

WEST VIRGINIA GAS COAL REGION

The class of gas coal known in the New York and Eastern markets as "West Virginia gas coal," is mined in Marion, Taylor, Ritchie and Preston counties, in that State, the mines being located near to the main line of the Baltimore and Ohio Railway. The coal is used for gas in the cities of the seaboard, and is very favorably spoken of. The distances to Baltimore are as follows: From Clarksburg, 301 miles: from Fairmount, 302 miles; from Newburg, 263 miles; from Tunnelton, 260 miles; from Cairo, 355 miles.

The veins are from six to eleven feet in thickness. Analyses of these coals have given the following results:

	Volatile matter.	Fixed carbon.	Ash.
Clarksburg, Main seam..................	56.74	41.66	1.60
" Cannel.....................	49.21	45.43	5.36

The trade to the seaboard began in the year 1868 with 165,772 tons. The business to date has been as below:

Year.	Tons.	Year.	Tons.	Year.	Tons.	Year.	Tons.
1868	165,772	1870	249,579	1872	217,569	1874	125,000
1869	269,153	1871	199,768	1873	190,673	1875	100,000

The only cause for a diminution of the product, lies in the fact, that of late years the B. & O. R. R. has not acted promptly in regard to freight charges at the opening of business, and the trade for Gas coal has been thrown into the hands of Pennsylvania coal producing companies.

In addition to the outlet eastward via B. & O. R. R., there is the Parkersburg route due west, crossing the Monongahela river at Clarksburg, and thence to the Ohio river at Parkersburg; and the Wheeling route north-westward, crossing the Monongahela at Fairmount, thence down the creek to the Ohio, and thence up the river to Wheeling. Both these branches enter the main coal measures near the crossing of the Monongahela above named, and traverse them to the Ohio. At Clarksburg and northward, down the valley of the Monongahela, is one of the richest coal regions of West Virginia. One of the beds in the neighborhood of this town measures from ten to twelve feet in thickness, with a thinner bed of more highly bituminous nature underlying; from some distance above Clarksburg, they may be followed with scarcely an interruption throughout the whole valley of the Monongahela northward to Pittsburgh.

THE CUMBERLAND, (MD.) REGION.

The Cumberland (George's Creek) coal field, located in Allegheny county, at the Western extremity of the State of Maryland, is the most important producer of Semi-Bituminous coal, of any district supplying the seaboard markets. The connections with the tide-water markets are via the B. & O. R. R., from the towns of Cumberland and Piedmont, 178 and 206 miles west from Baltimore; via the Chesapeake and Ohio Canal, following the Potomac river to Georgetown, 184 miles, and Alexandria, 191 miles from Cumberland.

The coal is bituminous, of superior quality; the vein worked is from seven to fourteen feet in thickness, but the full extent of the vein is seldom taken out, the roof being insecure. The mines are located at various distances from the shipping ports, say from 1½ to 20 miles from Piedmont, and from 11 to 33 from Cumberland.

The Consolidation Coal Company are the largest producers in the region, and own the Cumberland and Pennsylvania, and the Cumberland Branch lateral Railroads, but in point of shipments to tide-water they are far behind smaller companies; this company supplying the B. & O. Railroad.

In the year 1842 the Cumberland coal field sent its product to the tide-water markets over the branches of the B. & O. R. R., connecting with this field. In 1850 the Chesapeake and Ohio Canal was finished to Cumberland, Md.; and by it 4,042 tons were shipped in that year.

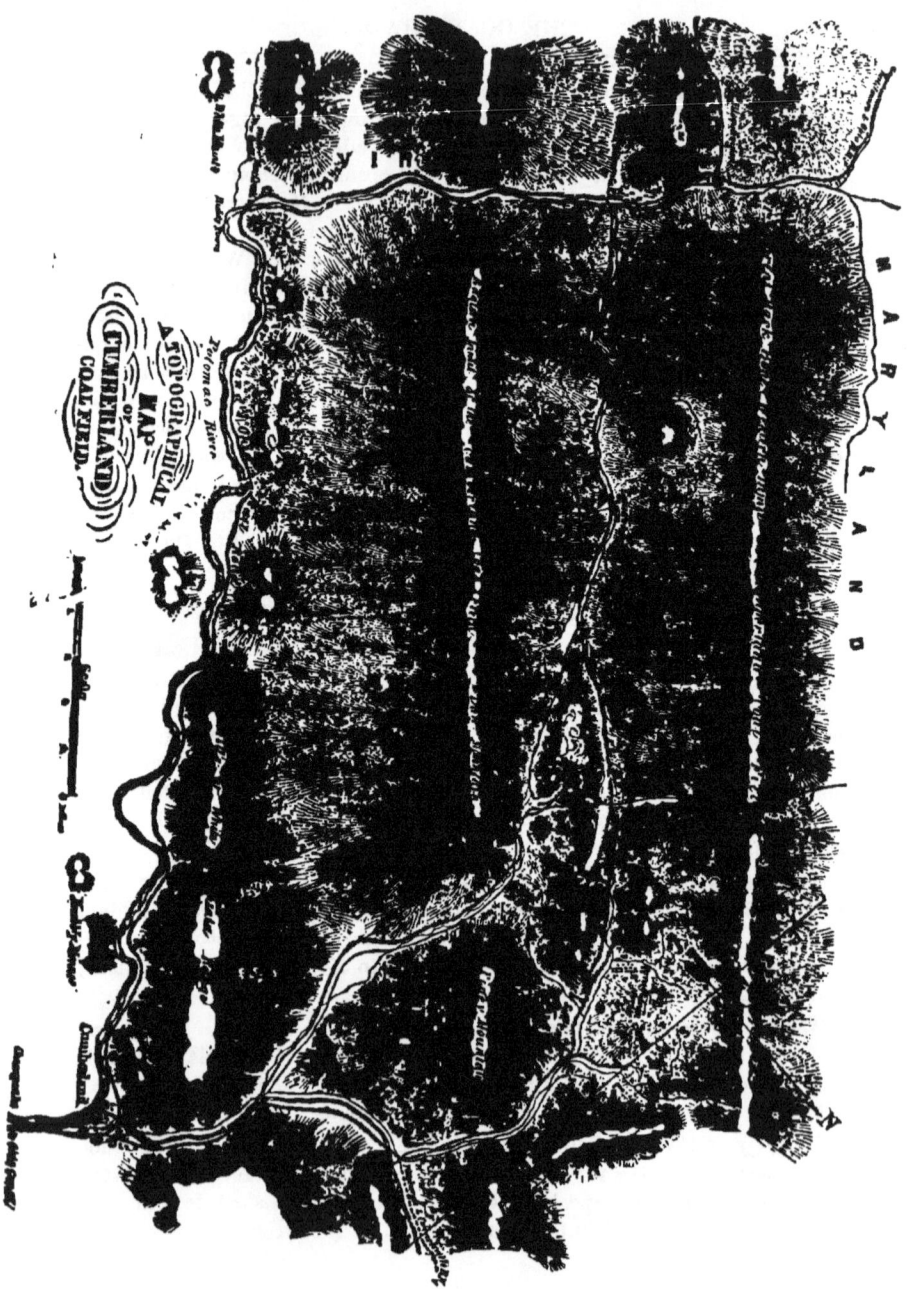

The production of Cumberland coal from 1842 to 1875, inclusive, was 28,681,454 tons, carried to market by the following routes, via B. & O. R. R., 18,850,671 tons; Chesapeake and Ohio Canal, 9,465,804 tons; and Pennsylvania State Line Railroad, 364,979 tons. The last named road was completed during the year 1872, connecting this region with the Pennsylvania Railroad, and 22,021 tons were carried over it in that year.

At the Piedmont end of this region, the Hampshire and Baltimore Company, and the Virginia Coal and Iron Company, connect by their own tramroads with the B. & O. Railway.

The Superintendent of the United States Armory at Springfield, Mass., made very thorough tests of the steam raising quality of this coal in the year 1871, each variety of three different classes of coal was used for six consecutive days, with the following reported results :

	Lackawanna.	Pittston.	Cumberland.
Pound per h. p. per hour...	4.01	4.04	3.43
Cost per gross ton...	$8.00	$7.58	$3.11
Cost per horse power...	1 5-10 cts.	1 4-10 cts.	1 2-10 cts.

And it is therefore alleged that the bituminous coal is the more economical fuel as a steam generator, making more heat and creating more power than harder coals.

The total Cumberland coal trade by railroad and canal from the beginning is shown in the following schedule :

Years.	Total by B. & O. R. R.	Total by C. & O. Canal.	P. S. Line branch to the P. R. R.
1842	1,708	....	....
1843	10,769	....	....
1844	14,590	....	....
1845	24,683	....	....
1846	29,795	....	....
1847	52,540	....	....
1848	79,371	....	....
1849	142,449	....	....
1850	192,806	4,042	....
1851	174,702	52,978	....
1852	265,180	65,719	....
1853	376,219	157,760	....
1854	508,866	183,845	....
1855	478,884	184,763	....
1856	5 2,534	2 4,121	....
1857	425,912	116,574	....
1858	395,415	234,861	....
1859	426,319	297,812	....
1860	435,481	295,678	....
1861	152,075	97,003	.
1862	218,950	9 6 4	..
1863	531,553	316,792	....
1864	359,234	185,741	.. ..
1865	560,233	245,2 2	....
1866	736,153	348,178	....
1867	735,609	456,153	....

THE COAL TRADE.

Years.	Total by B. & O. R. R.	Total by C. O. Canal.	P. S. Line branch to the P. R. R.
1868	848,118	482,325	....
1869	1,230,518	652,151	....
1870	1,112,938	604,151	....
1871	1,494,814	850,39	....
1872	1,637,368	816,103	22,031
1873	1,78,710	773,802	114,580
1874	1,576,160	767,054	67,671
1875	1,302,237	879,838	160,698

The following is interesting as showing the average price of Cumberland coal at Baltimore, the freight thence to Boston, and the price at which it was delivered at Boston during a series of years past :

Year	Average for year.	Av. freight to Boston.	Av. cost delivered in Boston.
1861	$3.44	$2.25	$5.69
1862	4.23	2.42	6.65
1863	5.57	3.29	8.83
1864	6.84	3.39	10.23
1865	7.57	3.79	11.36
1866	5.94	3.53	9.47
1867	4.97	2.68	7.65
1868	4.71	3.21	7.91
1869	4.97	2.83	7.80
1870	4.72	2.64	7.36
1871	4.72	2.73	7.45
1872	4.66	3.06	7.72
1873	4.84	3.17	8.01
1874	4.50	1.50	6.00
1875	4.20	1.30	5.50

During the year 1875, both coal and freights ruled very low, this enabled the district to hold up its product so nearly to that of former seasons ; there must necessarily have been a falling off, had not this been the case, as manufacturing was particularly dull during the year 1875.

The output during 1875 was produced by the following parties, and distributed by the routes named :

Names.	B. & O. R. R. Tons.	C. & O. Canal. Tons.	P. S. Line. Tons.	Local. Tons.	Total. Tons.
Consolidation	216,4 0	172,008	3,165	90,350	448,923
Maryland	63,208	196,104	......	2,000	261,309
New Central	91,652	69,914	97,184	97	268,847
Borden Mining	14,361	182,497	32,461	3,149	23,458
American	57,083	122,774	313	......	180,127
George's C. C. & I. Co.	140,958	24,378	......	1,021	166,357
Hamp. & Baltimore	9,082	53,690	......	167	62,985
" Va. Mines	90,690	......	......	110	90,800
Atlantic & George's Creek	118,199	230	24	3,463	124,916
Franklin	98,477	......	......	......	98,477
George's Creek Mining	85,881	......	......	......	85,881
Potomac	63,149	......	......	410	63,671
Swanton Mining Co.	66,499	......	27	143	64,559
Blaen Avon	3,041	57,241	......	......	60,282
Piedmont C. & I. Co.	54,819	......	524	......	55,343
Virginia C. & I. Co.	31,181	......	......	......	31,181
North Branch	26 425	......	......	65	26 490
New Reading	19,399	......	......	......	19,399
Davis Mines	5,866	......	......	......	5,866
Total	1,261,257	879,832	16,698	40,980	2,342,773

THE COAL TRADE.

Charges on the coal carried will be found in the "Rates of Transportation on Bituminous coals."

The entire length of this coal field is from 50 to 60 miles; viz., from the head waters of George's Creek, near Frostburg, about 15 miles to the north-east of Piedmont, to those of the north branch of the Potomac, some 30 miles to the south-east. The width of this valley averages 6 miles from outcrop to outcrop of the lower seams of coal. It is narrowest at the northern end, and widens out considerably at the southern. The total thickness of the coal containing strata is about 1400 feet, but this thickness does not pervade the entire area, as to the south of Piedmont and Bloomington the erosion has been greater, and it is only a few isolated hills that contain the upper seams of coal, and notably the "big" or fourteen feet seam.

In the entire thickness there are many seams of coal, but there are only five or six of a thickness of 3 feet or over, as follows: commencing with the lowest, known as the "Parker" and "Bluebaugh" veins at the northern end of the region, and which lie near the bottom of the formation, and are crossed by the river and railroad at Piedmont.

About 150 feet above is the 6 feet seam.
" 300   "   "   3   "   (Savage.)
" 380   "   "   5 " 8 inch seam.
" 600   "   "   5 " 9   "   "
" 850   "   " 14 " of "Big Vein."

The coal from the smaller veins will hardly come into use to a great extent, while that from the other and larger, continues to be offered at so low a rate, as at present.

The following table of production for the years 1874 and 1875 is of interest in this connection:

	1874-Tons.	1875-Tons.
Cumberland of Maryland	2,410,995	2,342,773
Clearfield of Pennsylvania	639,680	915,573
Snowshoe of Pennsylvania	65,540	82,496
Broad Top of Pennsylvania	226,608	288,488
McIntyre of Pennsylvania	158,917	164,507
Barclay of Pennsylvania	287,071	376,637
Blossburg of Pennsylvania	796,388	881,791
West Virginia Gas Coal	126,000	10,000
Imports of Bituminous Coal	473,024	441,600

CHICAGO, ILL.

This city is in direct rail and water communication with the Anthracite coal mines, and is therefore freely supplied at low rates. Contracts can be made at the present time with the responsible agent of the Anthracite Coal Association of Pennsylvania, for one or ten years to come, to deliver here the Lackawanna coal at $6.25 per net ton of 2,000 pounds, and the Lehigh coal for $7 per ton. This association owns their own roads from the mines to Buffalo and Oswego, and can lay down coal at the latter port for $3.75 per net ton. Freights the past year have been, from Oswego to Chicago, 95 cents to $1.65 per ton, and from Buffalo, from 40 cents to $1 per ton. This coal is largely exported from this city to St. Louis, Missouri, Kansas and Nebraska, also to Wisconsin, Iowa and Minnesota. The screenings from this coal can be had for $1 per ton. These are used for steam purposes.

It may be remarked that Chicago is now one of the most important markets in the country for soft coal, not only as regards its consumption for manufacturing and other purposes, but also as being the distributing point for a large section of the Northwest,

The receipts of coal at this city for the years 1874 and 1875, are shown below:

RECEIVED BY	TONS—1874.	TONS—1875.
Lake	661,583	748,706
Illinois and Michigan Canal	11,646	7,776
Chicago and Northwestern Railroad	2,092	5,564
Illinois Central Railroad	35,921	38,266
Chicago, Rock Island and Pacific Railroad	18,135	31,583
Chicago, Burlington and Quincy Railroad	27,661	5,821
Chicago and Alton Railroad	254,030	278,006
Chicago, Det. oit and Vincennes Railroad	147,701	205,530
Lake Shore and Michigan Southern	455	778
Pittsburgh, Fort Wayne and Chicago Railroad	64,314	112,609
Pittsburgh, Chicago and St Louis Railroad	133,232	150,349
Baltimore and Ohio Railroad	2,726	57,900
Michigan Central Railroad	....	3,266
Total	1,359,496	1,641,488

The ton weight designated in these tables is that of 2,000 pounds.

The shipments from the city are by railway, mainly by the Chicago and Northwestern Railroad, to points in the Western States.

The following tables evidence the growth of the coal trade at this city:

RECEIPTS BY LAKE.

ANTHRACITE.		BITUMINOUS.	
Years.	Tons.	Years.	Tons.
1870	340,730	1870	181,859
1872	495,765	1872	90,884
1873	536,637	1873	199,107
1874	404,383	1874	257,200
1875	474,512	1875	365,617

THE COAL TRADE.

RECEIPTS OF ALL KINDS OF COAL.

Years.	Tons.	Years.	Tons.
1852	46,208	1855	109,676
1853	38,548	1856	98,000
1854	56,774	1857	171,279

Years.	By Lake.	By Rail	By Canal	Total tons.
1858	76,571	10,719	2,364	87,720
1859	111,506	11,766	7,922	131,204
1860	117,646	6,218	7,216	131,080
1861	168,679	2,407	12,808	184,049
1862	196,099	7,861	15,648	218,423
1863	244,624	12,066	27,506	244,196
1864	251,088	43,991	25,346	322,275
1865	288,771	41,093	15,060	344,904
1866	385,906	64,675	22,612	406,198
1867	391,313	140,319	14,676	546,308
1868	450,137	197,169	10,945	698,248
1869	510,676	279,786	8,296	799,600
1870	522,580	364,894	......	887,474
1871	513,253	662,043	4,176	1,081,472
1872	586,585	604,226	7,213	1,398,094
1873	737,944	913,205	17,118	1,668,267
1874	661,848	636,267	11,646	1,339,696
1875	748,706	865,004	7,778	1,641,498

SHIPMENTS OF ALL KINDS OF COAL FROM CHICAGO.

Years.	Tons.	Years.	Tons.
1852	1,441	1864	16,779
1853	2,999	1865	94,190
1854	3,948	1866	34,190
1855	12,152	1867	69,170
1856	16,161	1868	83,299
1857	33,942	1869	95,690
1858	15,641	1870	110,467
1859	19,866	1871	96,833
1860	20,864	1872	177,867
1861	20,196	1873	943,627
1862	12,947	1874	202,973
1863	16,245	1875	345,517

Details of the business for the year 1875, are shown below:

	SHIPMENTS.		RECEIPTS.	
	Anthracite. Tons.	Bituminous. Tons.	Anthracite. Tons.	Bituminous. Tons.
By Lake	677	51	474,612	273,894
Illinois and Michigan Canal		7,884	......	7,778
Chicago and Northwestern Railroad	56,000	180,694	......	564
Illinois Central Railroad	18,597	......	......	38,298
Chicago, Rock Island and Pacific R'd	23,204	......	......	31,893
Chicago, Burlington and Quincy R. R.	29,991	......	......	5,321
Chicago and Alton Railroad	14,070	......	......	278,896
Chicago, Detroit and Vincennes R. R.	832	......	......	705,330
C. M. & St. P. R. R.	......	36,656	......	......
Chicago and Pacific Railroad	2,500	2,040	......	......
Michigan Central Railroad	......	948	3,266	......
Lake Shore and Michigan Southern	......	784	779	......
Pittsburgh, Fort Wayne and Chicago	1,320	......	......	112,600
Pittsburgh, Chicago and St. Louis	1,102	......	......	130,540
Baltimore and Ohio Railroad	......	365	......	57,900

SAN FRANCISCO, CAL.

The statement given below will indicate at a glance the increased consumption of the several varieties at San Francisco.

	1869.	1870.	1871.	1872.
Foreign	109,000	135,164	113,483	174,212
Eastern	38,600	30,820	13,291	29,669
Domestic	184,100	167,183	188,420	230,586
Total	331,700	333,177	315,194	434,467
		1873.	1874.	1875.
Foreign		151,884	227,952	255,700
Eastern		27,167	29,739	29,138
Domestic		221,034	2:1,257	253,231
Total		431,039	381,947	538,209

Details of the business for 1875, are as below :

Foreign : Australian, 136,869 tons ; English, 57,849 tons ; Vancouver, 61,072 tons.

Eastern ; Anthracite, 18,810 tons ; Cumberland, 10,328 tons.

Domestic : Mt. Diablo. 142,808 tons ; Coos Bay, 32,869 tons ; Bellingham Bay, 10,445 tons ; Seattle, 67,106 tons ; Rocky Mountain, 53 tons.

The ton weight is that of 2240 lbs.—

The following is of interest, as showing the relative value of the coals found on the Pacific coast compared with the coal from the Cumberland region in Maryland :

	A	B	C	D	E	F
Alaska	7.94	7.96	60.0	40.0	12.3	5.41
Coos Bay	10.24	7.35	69.7	39.3	6.2	6.91
Seattle	8.38	9.57	63.0	37.0	10.6	5.71
Black Diamond	8.3	8.73	51.6	48.4	8.0	5.71
Bellingham Bay	10.68	5.51	67.0	33.0	16.0	7.21
California Anthracite	9.70	6.12	83.6	11.4	5.0	6.61
Cumberland, Maryland	13.92	3.52	88.2	11.8	3.2	9.28

EXPLANATION.—*A*, heating power, one pound water; *B*, sulphur to ton, in pounds; *C*, coke per cent ; *D*, Volatile matter ; *E*, Ash per cent ; *F*, relative value per pound.

ST. LOUIS, MO.

By far the largest proportion of the Bituminous coal received at this city is from the Belleville district, in St. Clair county, Illinois ; the principal seam worked is five to seven feet in thickness, and is economically mined. Analysis of this coal shows, Water 6 ; Volatile matter 38.8 ; Fixed Carbon 55.2 ; Ash 5.

The Iron Mountain Railroad brings the Semi-Anthracite coal known as the "Spadra" from Arkansas to this city, a description of its qualities will be found in the proper place.

The following statement shows the coal trade of St. Louis for 1874 and 1875 :

THE COAL TRADE.

ROUTES OF TRANSPORTATION.	1874. TONS.	1875. TONS.
Belleville and Southern Illinois Railroad	311,105	250,736
Illinois and St. Louis Railroad	194,966	264,624
Ohio and Mississippi Railroad	161,390	160,467
St. Louis and Southeastern Railroad	161,766	174,272
St. Louis, Vandalia, Terre Haute, and Ind. Railroad	121,445	121,012
Indianapolis and St. Louis Railroad	24,390	12,776
Cairo and St. Louis Narrow-gauge	84,150	107,164
Chicago, Alton and St. Louis Railroad	6,500	1,750
Toledo, Wabash and Western Railroad	2,100	14,250
Rockford, Rock Island and St. Louis Railroad	1,500	1,500
Iron Mountain and Southern Railroad	1,755	995
St. Louis County wagon receipts (estimated)	64,000	75,000
Ohio and Cumberland River (Barges)	15,415	63,190
Lower Mississippi River	2,000	1,500
Illinois River	1,300	1,500
Pittsburgh gas coals	41,000	50,000
Other sources	500	1,500
Total receipts	1,194,622	1,274,819

Tons of 2,000 lbs ; 25 bushels of 80 lbs. each, to the ton.——

BUFFALO, N. Y.

The distribution of the coal received here is divided into city trade for family use, rolling mills, furnaces, manufactories and gas works ; interior trade for gas works, family use and manufacturing purposes ; and all points of the West are supplied principally with Anthracite, which is taken by vessels from this port to Chicago, Milwaukee, Duluth, etc.

The receipts for a series of years have been as below :

Year.	BITUMINOUS.			ANTHRACITE.	
	By Lake.	By Canal.	By L. S. & M. S. R. R.	By Canal.	By Rail.
1863	71,323	12,551	....	128,319	....
1864	65,924	36,287	....	154,214	....
1865	69,141	43,722	....	143,993	....
1866	85,142	62,172	....	248,716	....
1867	101,107	67,124	....	292,719	....
1868	91,457	73,598	....	318,350	....
1869	99,460	108,972	....	112,914	197,000
1870	94,796	168,437	....	177,027	254,000
1871	88,511	80,660	76,063	109,183	290,000
1872	78,879	95,500	109,397	190,904	320,000
1873	87,784	125,000	190,000	285,044	479,8%
1874	67,467	70,000	140,000	202,202	294,000
1875	82,767	45,100	250,000	259,200	800,000

The shipments of Bituminous eastward by canal from Buffalo were as below :

1863	20,125	1869	64,680
1864	80,043	1870	65,940
1865	38,263	1871	60,522
1866	50,202	1872	63,198
1867	57,495	1873	68,210
1868	59,766	1874	46,796
	1875	25,100	

There was 80,000 tons of Blossburg Semi-Bituminous received in 1873, 50,000 tons in 1874, and 75,000 tons in 1875 by railroad. The amount of Anthracite that was shipped westward, via the lakes, 510,443 tons in 1873, 344,500 in 1874, and 339,722 tons in 1875. There was 60,000 tons of Blossburg Semi-Bituminous shipped west, via the lakes in 1873, 40,000 in 1874 and 50,000 tons in 1875.

Freights ranged from 50 cents to $1.00 per ton to Chicago, Ills.

The ton weight in use here is that of 2,000 lbs.

MOBILE, ALA.

The Mobile *Register* in its annual review dated September 1st., 1875, says: The past year, similar to the previous season, has been very unsatisfactory to our coal dealers; the demand has been principally for household purposes, and in consequence of the exceedingly mild winter, consumption has been moderate. The boats, presses and manufactories continue to use pine wood (lightwood), which can be freely obtained at about $3.00 per cord—making a fuel so cheap as to prevent the substitution of coal until it can be furnished at a considerably reduced price from present rates. We anticipated in our last annual statement the opening of a trade in Alabama coal with Cuba and Texas, but as yet no shipments have been made, although samples have been sent to Mexico, Cuba and St. Thomas, and our dealers have encouragement to hope that they will soon receive test orders. The railroads freight the Alabama coal at as low a figure as they can afford, yet the cost is too high for very successful competition with the Cumberland and Anthracite coals. If our upper rivers were made navigable, good steam coal could be supplied at this port from $3.00 to $4.00 per ton, and a large trade would soon be established. The following are the comparative receipts for four years:

	1872.	1873.	1874.	1855.
Pennsylvania and English	8,359	8,009	5,830	4,176
Alabama	1,561	1,166	1,154	1,501

PITTSBURGH, PA.

The amount of business that is done at this city in coal and coke, including that sent to other points, amounts to 4,350,000 tons (of 2,000 pounds) per year.

The business of the Monongahela slack-water navigation in 1875 amounted to 2,046,967 tons of coal and 38,308 tons of coke.

During last year there was quite a business done in Anthracite coal.

The rapid growth of the coke trade of Pittsburgh and vicinity is a most significant illustration of its industrial development. Of this trade, what is known as Connellsville coke forms a large part, and will continue to do so. It is mined in Fayette county, Pa. It is stated that an acre will yield, over and above the pillars, if properly mined, 13,300 tons. It weighs 80 lbs. to a bushel, and when properly coked, 100 bushels of coal produce 125 bushels of coke, and the coke weighs 40 pounds to a bushel; that is, a given quantity of the coal gains one quarter in bulk and loses three-eighths of its weight, or 100 pounds of coal makes 62½ pounds of coke. This coke has become very celebrated not only about Pittsburgh, but throughout the Western States, where it is extensively used for foundry purposes in melting pig iron, selling in competition with Lehigh coal. It is used in blast furnaces for smelting iron from the ore, and is sometimes mixed with the

Western coals. It is also an excellent fuel for locomotive use. Its freedom from sulphur has given this coke the reputation of being the best known. An analysis made by J. B. Britton of a sample of Connellsville coke, average of forty-nine pieces, shows :

Moisture	.49	Phosphoric acid	.08
Ash	11.23	Carbon	87.44
Sulphur	.09		

The ash of the coke contained 47 per cent of silica and 47 per cent of alumina.

The receipts during the years 1874 and 1875 are as below :

BITUMINOUS COAL IN TONS OF 2,000 LBS.

Route of Transportation.	1874.	1875.
Allegheny Valley Railroad	240,165	271,725
Castle Shannon Railroad	122,925	97,322
Pittsburgh and Connellsville Railroad	453,976	336,000
Pennsylvania Railroad	533,777	331,913
Pittsburgh, Charleston and West Virginia Railroad	30,096	43,930
Pittsburgh, Cincinnati, and St. Louis Railroad	210,222	249,891
Saw Mill Run Railroad	89,676	90,047
Monongahela Slack-water	2,196,158	2,046,967
West Pennsylvania Railroad. Estimated	194,008	150,000
Total	4,021,000	3,616,678
COKE IN TONS OF 2,000 LBS.		
Connellsville Railroad	630,727	540,000
Pennsylvania Railroad	512,783	422,918
West Pennsylvania Railroad	46,163	45,000
Monongahela Slack-water	32,575	38,304
Total	1,222,056	1,036,222

The above schedule was prepared by the *American Manufacturer.*

Grand Total coal and coke receipts ; for 1874, 5,243,056 tons, for 1875, 4,662,889 tons.

BALTIMORE, MD.

At this city an extensive business in coal, both Anthracite and Bituminous, is done. At Locust Point, the terminus of the Baltimore and Ohio Railroad, on the environs of this fine city, is the shipping point for immense quantities of Bituminous coal from the Cumberland region of Maryland, the Gas coal regions of West Virginia, the Somerset county mines and the Youghiogheny Gas coal of Pennsylvania.

The highest price at which the Cumberland coal has been sold at Baltimore, was in March, 1865, when the price was $14 per ton ; it rapidly declined, until, in December of the same year, the price was but $7 40 per ton. The trade in Anthracite at present is entirely local, none being shipped from Baltimore to other and more distant points.

There are some 350,000 tons of Anthracite received yearly at Baltimore, by the following routes : From Millersburg, Pa., 112 miles, the Lykens

Valley Red Ash; from Sunbury, Pa., 138 miles, the White Ash; by Susquehanna tide water canal; from Port Richmond, Philadelphia.

Little or no Lehigh coal reaches Baltimore. The Anthracite is usually of good quality. All the sales are 2,240 pounds to the ton. Anthracite sold as high as $13.50 per ton or Lump coal, in May, 1865.

The gross rates of transportation, on coal for shipment at Locust Point over the Baltimore and Ohio Railroad, du ing 1875, were as below:

```
Cumberland to Locust Point..................................................$2.05
Piedmont to Locust Point.....................................................2.40
Newburg to Locust Point......................................................4.25
Clarksburg and Fairmount to Locust Point....................................4.75
```

per ton of 2,000 lbs., with a drawback off Gas coal reshipped North and East.

The shipments from Baltimore of Cumberland coal to foreign ports were as below:

```
1871..................20,207      1873..................59,546
1872..................54,363      1874..................70,675
            1875..................33,460
```

The Northern Central Railroad took 276,784 tons of Anthracite to Baltimore in 1875, against 232,938 in 1874, 242,754 tons in 1873 and 244,757 tons in 1872.

The amount of West Virginia Gas coal that is received averages about 200,000 tons annually, being 217,569 tons in 1872, and 190,673 tons in 1873 There were also shipped during 1874 some 30,000 tons of Youghiogheny Gas coal, and 60,000 tons in 1875; received from Western Pennsylvania by the Pittsburgh and Connellsville branch of the Baltimore and Ohio Railroad.

The Pennsylvania Railroad carried the coal from the Clearfield region, to Baltimore in 1875, by its Northern Central line.

The following schedule shows the business of the Baltimore and Ohio Railroad Company, giving the disposition of the coal that paid freight (coal for the use of the company not included):

Fiscal Years.	Received at Locust Point.	To Baltimore.	Line Trade.
1862	150,937	6,740	978
1863	277,505	26,106	3,936
1864	302,277	56,191	1,103
1865	353,434	49,396	5,340
1866	620,688	77,856	20,967
1867	629,946	58,377	7,615
1868	696,465	39,766	29,780
1869	1,187,306	136,704	33,910
1870	1,069,390	113,929	36,319
1871	1,433,816	113,286	39,500
1872	1,482,240	60,630	118,359
1873	1,806,529	65,694	147,195

BUSINESS OF 1874.—The Baltimore and Ohio Company state that the amount of coal carried for the year ending in 1874 was 1,407,377 tons, but do not furnish the details of distribution, or, as to how much was Cumberland, and West Virginia Gas, or Youghiogheny coal. The year of the Baltimore and Ohio Railroad ends October 31.

CINCINNATI, OHIO.

There is an increasing business done in coal at this city. The qualities received embrace Youghiogheny from the neighborhood of Pittsburgh, Pa.; the Pomeroy from the vicinity of Pomeroy, Ohio; Hocking Valley, Ohio; the Kanawha from West Virginia, including the Splint, Bituminous and Cannel; and the Anthracite from Pennsylvania.

Of Anthracite coal, the quantity consumed in this city is small, not exceeding during the past year, 248,750 bushels. The price delivered to dealers is about $9.87 per ton.

The shipments of coal from this city to interior towns have decreased during 1874-75 amounting to 5,002,500 bushels against 5,933,100 bushels in 1873-74, and 4,472,400 bushels in 1872-73.

The following table shows the receipts of coal of the various kinds at this city.

KINDS.	BUSHELS.	
	1873-74.	1874-75.
Youghiogheny	24,014,681	24,225,002
Ohio River	} 10,396,153	4,277,437
Kanawha		4,476,619
Cannel	716,000	569,359
Anthracite	112,000	248,750
Muskingum Valley		312,000
Hocking Valley		636,000
Other receipts		649,250
Totals	35,234,834	35,394,300

The following table shows the average annual quotation for Youghiogheny coal, delivered.

YEAR.	CTS. PER BUSHEL.	YEAR.	CTS. PER BUSHEL.
1863-64	28.24	1869-70	15.27
1864-65	26.13	1870-71	18.52
1865-66	24.42	1871-72	22.65
1866-67	17.86	1872-73	20.72
1867-68	22.01	1873-74	16.04
1868-69	14.00	1874-75	14.00

It must be remembered, however, that this is by no means the average price of the coal consumed, for these averages depend on the regular weekly quotations, and to take them as the measure of the average price, would be to assume that equal quantities were consumed at the different seasons of the year, which would be fallacious. For comparative purposes, these figures are the best that can under the circumstances be furnished, but for absolute cost they are unsafe criteria.

THE COAL TRADE.

A noticeable feature of the coal trade in this city is the more general use of coke as a fuel for the household. While the quantity used for manufacturing has, from the very nature of the cause, suffered material diminution, this has found at least partial compensation in the growing demand for other purposes. Crushed coke, a new article of fuel, which was introduced a short time ago, has been largely consumed, and has been shipped in considerable quantities to other cities. The business for the year is placed at 2,675,000 bushels, compared with 2,850,000 during the preceding year. Gas coke has ranged from 7 to 8 cents per bushel at the works, with an extra charge for delivery of from 2 to 4 cents per bushel, according to location. The average quotation per bushel during the year, for the various kinds of coke, has been as follows :—City manufactured, at yard, 11 cents, delivered, 13.1 ; Gas House, at yard, 7-75, delivered, 10.7 ; Connellsville, delivered, 15.58 ; McKeesport, delivered, 11.13 ; Crushed, at yard, 11.25, delivered, 14.25.

While Youghiogheny has not varied much in quantity, and the demand for Ohio River coal has fallen off, the quantity of Kanawha coal received has steadily increased. A new feature of the business in this city is the completion of the arrangements for the receipt of the Hocking Valley coal over the Marietta and Cincinnati Railroad. Extensive and permanent depots have been established at Brighton Station, on the Cincinnati and Baltimore Railway, and the work of receipt and distribution has been successfully established. As to what effect the receipt of coal by rail, on an extensive scale, will hereafter have upon the market, remains to be seen ; but it will, at any rate, test the foundation for the hopes entertained by many for years that the solution of the question of low prices and equable supply was to be found through the instrumentality of the railroads.

The following table will show the number of bushels of coal of all kinds, received at Cincinnati, for the years named :

YEAR.	BUSHELS.	YEAR.	BUSHELS.
1853-54	8,159,000	1864-65	16,467,023
1854-55	10,336,000	1865-66	16,022,990
1855-56	7,500,000	1866-67	18,446,226
1856-57	14,500,000	1867-68	17,500,000
1857-58	15,000,000	1868-69	25,500,000
1858-59	12,392,701	1869-70	30,800,000
1859-60	14,600,000	1870-71	22,972,000
1860-61	12,500,000	1871-72	30,790,796
1861-62	8,500,000	1872-73	37,274,497
1862-63	6,000,000	1873-74	35,234,534
1863-64	15,975,366	1874-75	35,360,800

It is safe to calculate the bushel at eighty pounds, which would give twenty-eight to the ton of 2,240 lbs.

For the figures given above we are indebted to Col. Sydney D. Maxwell, Superintendent of the Cincinnati Chamber of Commerce.

PROVIDENCE, R. I.

The total amount of coal reported as received at this port during the year 1875, was 603,510 tons, of which amount 602,847 tons was domestic and only 663 tons foreign. The total receipts of coal for 1874 were 539,169 tons, of which 532,564 tons were domestic and 6,604 tons foreign; showing a gain of 70,282 tons of domestic, and a loss of 5,941 tons of foreign. Total receipts for 1873 were 634,112 tons domestic, 3,232 foreign, in all 637,344 tons, or 33,835 tons more than during last year. For 1872, 623,842 tons domestic, 9,454 tons foreign, total, 633,387, or 29,877 tons more, in all, than in 1875. For the year 1871, 504,006 tons domestic, 13,900 tons foreign; total, 517,996 tons, or 85,514 tons less than during the year 1875.

NEW ORLEANS, LA.

The *Price Current* in its annual review for the year ending Sept. 1st, 1875, says:

"The coal brought to this market is almost exclusively Pittsburgh coal. The flats and barges are towed by powerful towboats built expressly for that purpose. The towing between Pittsburgh and Louisville depends on the state of the river. When the stage of water is too low for navigation, which it frequently is for weeks; and even months, the supplies at the lower points become deficient and prices naturally advance, often reaching very high figures. The coal flats and barges sent to New Orleans are generally dropped at Willow Grove, near Greenville, just above the city, where they are superintended for the owners or agents. When a boat or barge is wanted a small city tugboat is sent to tow it to the city, or to its destination on the coast. The aggregate consumption for six years—1869, 1870, 1871, 1872, 1873, 1874, were as below:

		Bbls.	Tons.
Boats	1,837	15,614,500	1,419,500
Barges	569	2,560,500	232,772
Total	2,406	18,175,000	1,652,272
AVERAGE FOR ONE YEAR.			
Boats	306	2,501,000	236,454
Barges	95	427,500	38,862
Total	401	2,928,500	275,317

The largest amount of coal consumed in the past six years, was 301,555 tons in 1869, and the least, 248,136 tons in 1874."

Messrs. C. A. Miltenberger & Co., give the following as the consumption of Pittsburgh coal at this port:

THE COAL TRADE.

	Bbls.		Bbls.
Consumption 1869	3,317,099	Consumption 1873	2,841,500
" 1870	3,203,600	" 1874	2,749,500
" 1871	2,112,000	" 1875	2,448,000
" 1872	2,991,500		

The coal sent to planters below the city is included in the consumption, while that left on the coast above is not considered.
French Creeks are classed as barges, and Hulls as boats.
Average contents, boats about 9,000 bbls. Barges 4,500 bbls.

The average cost of carrying coal from Pittsburgh to New Orleans, (the round trip) is stated at 1-64th of a cent per ton, per mile.

RICHMOND, VA.

Our friends at this city kindly forward the following statistics of the coal trade for the years 1874 and 1875.

Receipts.	Tons, 1874.	Tons, 1875.
Via Richmond and Danville Railroad, Chesterfield County coal	18,690	14,500
Via Richmond and Petersburg Railroad (Clover Hill), Chesterfield County coal	17,104	16,592
Via River Potomac, and Fredericksburg Railroad, Henrico County coal	2,000	2,500
Via canal, Carbonite, coke and coal	20,440	19,301
Via dock (Cumberland and Anthracite), Northern coal	69,088	49,700
Via Chesapeake and Ohio Railroad, to James River	75,621	80,000
" " city		20,000

COAL AT BOSTON, MASS.

The comparative receipts for the years 1874 and 1875 are shown below:

From	Tons, 1874.	Tons, 1875.
Alexandria, Virginia	86,705	97,097
Georgetown, District of Columbia	27,753	20,567
Philadelphia, Pennsylvania	578,432	623,245
Baltimore, Maryland	197,513	168 798
Other places (New York, etc.)	235,113	290,271
Great Britain	2,780	2,738
Nova Scotia	48,658	29,706
Totals	1,175,954	1,233,022

The receipts of foreign and domestic coal at this port have been as follows:

Years.	Foreign. Tons.	Domestic. Tons.	Years.	Foreign. Tons.	Domestic. Tons.
1875	32,444	1,200,578	1868	103,901	742,491
1874	51,483	1,125,516	1867	117,440	680,221
1873	87,700	1,076,673	1866	159,380	676,376
1872	90,739	1,065,781	1865	209,225	635,917
1871	109,013	822,808	1864	168,786	516,665
1870	115,022	819,890	1863	180,443	589,921
1869	110,466	764,017			

These figures include all the coal going to this port, both for the home trade, and for the points reached by the railroads centering here.

The Boston *Commercial* and *Shipping List* gives the following as the following as the highest and lowest prices of Anthracite and Provincial coal, at the city of Boston.

Years.	Anthracite, per ton.		Nova Scotia, per ton.	
1875	$7.18	@$9.03	$6.25	$6.25
1874	7.00	9.00	5.75	7.75
1873	8.00	10.00	7.00	9.00
1872	7.00	10.00	6.00	8.50
1871	7.00	10.80	5.75	7.00
1870	7.00	11.00	5.75	7.25
1849	7.50	11.00	7.25	9.00
1848	7.00	12.80	7.50	9.00
1847	7.50	10.60	7.25	9.25
1846	9.00	12.00	7.50	9.50
1845	5.75	17.00	6.25	18.00

CLEVELAND, OHIO.

This city receives as fine and varied an assortment of Bituminous coal as any city in the world. A great many coal basins—in fact, nearly all the Ohio formation, as well as most of the coals lying west of the Alleghany Mountains, in Pennsylvania—here find a market and a distributing point for the West, Northwest, Eastern and Canada trade,

The great number of vessels employed in the iron ore and lumber trade naturally seek coal as a back freight for ballast, which enables Cleveland to place coal in distant ports, like Chicago, Milwaukee and Lake Superior, at mere nominal rates. The bulk of the business has been developed within the last fifteen years, and, taking the rapid growth of the manufacturing interests in the West into consideration, it is safe to presume that the trade has not yet reached its ultimate proportions.

The total receipts of coal at Cleveland from 1828 to 1852 amounted to 662,862 tons, and increasing from thirty tons in 1828 to 137,926 tons in 1852, mined as below :

Year.	District.	Tons for the year.
1828	Tallmadge	30
1830	Tallmadge	708
1830	Tallmadge	1,178
1840	Tallmadge, New Castle, Trenton	6,028
1850	Tallmadge, Clinton, New Castle, Youngstown, Cuyahoga Falls, Girard and Rochester	83,850
1851	Tallmadge, Clinton, New Castle, Youngstown, Cuyahoga Falls, Girard and Rochester	107,135
1852	Tallmadge, Clinton, New Castle, Youngstown, Cuyahoga Falls, Girard and Rochester	137,956

The canal from Akron was opened July 4, 1828, and during that year the thirty tons of coal sent to Cleveland was received by this canal route. The coal was taken from the mines to the canal with teams, to be shipped, and the business was continued in this way until 1832, when the canal reached the coal fields near Massillon, which were on its banks. The receipts by this route represents the consumption of coal at Cleveland up to 1838. It was not until after this, and after the Briar Hill coal began to reach this place, in 1843, that lake steamers could be induced to use it. Since 1845 it has supplanted wood on the steamers of the lower lakes.

Until 1845 the entire trade of the lakes in Bituminous coal was in the hands of Cleveland dealers. About this time, possibly a year or two earlier, Erie began to ship coal, the joint receipts from the interior of the two places being only 45,136 tons.

The Bituminous coals received at Cleveland may be classed as follows:

Briar Hill or Block coal from the Mahoning region—reach Cleveland via A. & G. W. Railroad.

Massillon coal region—via C. & P. Railway and Canal.

Tuscarawas coal region—via L. S. & T. V. Railway, and C. & P. Railway.

Salinesville and Hammondsville region—via C. & P. Railway.

Sterling—via C. & P. Railway.

Pittsburgh coal region—via C. & P. Railway.

Straitsville—via C. C. & I. Railway.

Hocking—via C C. & I. Railway.

Statistics in regard to the tonnage have not been very carefully preserved, but the following table may be relied upon as not being over-estimated, as it is compiled from the returns of the different transportation companies.

	Receipts.	Shipments.	Used in Cleveland.
1865	465,550	236,000	229,550
1866	583,457	295,280	289,127
1867	663,026	334,027	334,999
1868	759,104	392,928	359,176
1869	922,757	495,800	426,957
1870	904,600	482,306	422,210
1871	1,165,940	683,765	532,715
1872	1,349,160	745,595	602,585
1873	1,599,212	854,862	744,350
1874	1,099,000	500,000	599,000

The amount of Anthracite coal received at this city is very small, amounting to but 36,358 tons in 1874. The amount of *shipments* in 1875 was 529,211 tons coastwise, and 140,637 tons to the British Provinces.

The ton designated is that of 2000 lbs.

IMPORTS AND EXPORTS OF COAL.

By the courtesy of Dr. Edward Young, Chief of the Bureau of Statistics, at Washington, D. C., we are enabled to give the following in regard to the imports and exports of coal into and from the United States:

IMPORTS.		EXPORTS.	
Years.	Tons.	Years.	Tons.
1870	420,066	1870	397,918
1871	443,955	1871	377,961
1872	400,62*	1872	401,078
1873	454,015	1873	864,688
1874	443,028	1874	762,402
1875	441,600	1875	819,345

Details for the fiscal year ending June 30, 1875, are as below:

	DOMESTIC EXPORTS.		IMPORTS.
	Bituminous.	Anthracite.	Bituminous.
Argentine Republic		228	
Brazil	1,169	1,220	104
Central American States	1	36	
Chili	1,220	283	
China		4,066	
Danish West Indies	8,946	556	11
France			488
French West Indies	8,868	105	26
Miquelon, Lang.ay and St. Pierre		79	
Germany			725
England			108,154
Scotland			14,352
Nova Scotia, New Brunswick, &c	2,512	18,990	127,800
Quebec, Ontario, &c	137,653	245,726	115
British Columbia	72	5	28,923
Newfoundland and Labrador		522	
British West Indies	2,577	778	17
British Guiana			1
Hong Kong		743	2
British Australasia		716	129,300
Hayti		67	
Italy			9
Japan		1,330	
Mexico	3,134	4,118	8
Peru		50	5
Azore, Maderia and Cape Verde		10	12
Sandwich Islands	68	2,975	
Cuba	33,005	21,313	201
Porto Rico	155	23	
Spanish Possessions in Africa		4	
" " all other	150		
Turkey in Africa			5
U. S. of Columbia	14,107	11,078	15
Uruguay	249		4
Venezuela	90	95	
All other countries and ports in Africa		129	
Total	208,180	316,166	441,600

N. B.—The Foreign Re-Exports during the fiscal year 1875 amounted to 5 tons—$110.

NOVA SCOTIA.

Nova Scotia coal was admitted into the United States free of duty during the years 1854 to 1865, and the average annual production of those twelve years was only 333,427 tons. A monopoly of these regions was granted to the Duke of York in 1826, but it was relinquished in 1857. The most important regions are Pictou, and Sydney or Cape Breton, as will be seen from the tables of the production. New Brunswick posseses a mine of what is called Albertite, a variety of asphalt which yields 100 gallons of crude oil to the ton, or 14,500 cubic feet of gas. It was discovered in 1849. The Pictou field is said to contain some 28 square miles, but the available space for working is much less. The most extensive is the Cape Breton field. It extends about thirty-five miles along the coast, and ranges from four to five miles in width.

Mr. H. S. Poole, Government Inspector of Mines, furnishes the following summary of the coal sales of Nova Scotia from 1785 to 1874.

Years.	Tons.	Years.	Tons.
1785 to 1790	14,349	1831 to 1840	839,981
1791 " 1800	51,048	1841 " 1850	1,533,798
1801 " 1810	70,452	1851 " 1860	2,399,829
1811 " 1820	91,527	1861 " 1870	4,927,339
1821 " 1830	140,320	1871 " 1874	3,012,565

The above table is probably as nearly correct as can now be determined, and if 13 per cent be allowed for colliery consumption 1,700,622 tons must be added making the total quantity actually raised 14,782,330 tons.

The number of tons actually raised during a term of years is shown in the following schedule:

Year.	Tons.
1864	563,102
1865	715,786
1866	661,098
1867	517,425
1868	462,184
1869	578,032
1870	623,769
1871	673,242
1872	880,950
1873	1,051,407
1874	872,720
1875	781,165

The colliery consumption for 1875, was 15 per cent or 124,110 tons.—

During the year 1875, freights from the Provinces ruled very low, and prices at the shipping ports were also low, yet the output was less even than in 1874, and a great decrease from the business of 1873; this is no doubt owing to the low prices of American coals, and the general dullness of manufacturing of every description, during that year.

The average prices of Nova Scotia coal, delivered at Boston, Mass., together with the amount of Nova Scotia coal received into the whole United States, for fiscal year ending June 30th, are stated in the following schedule:

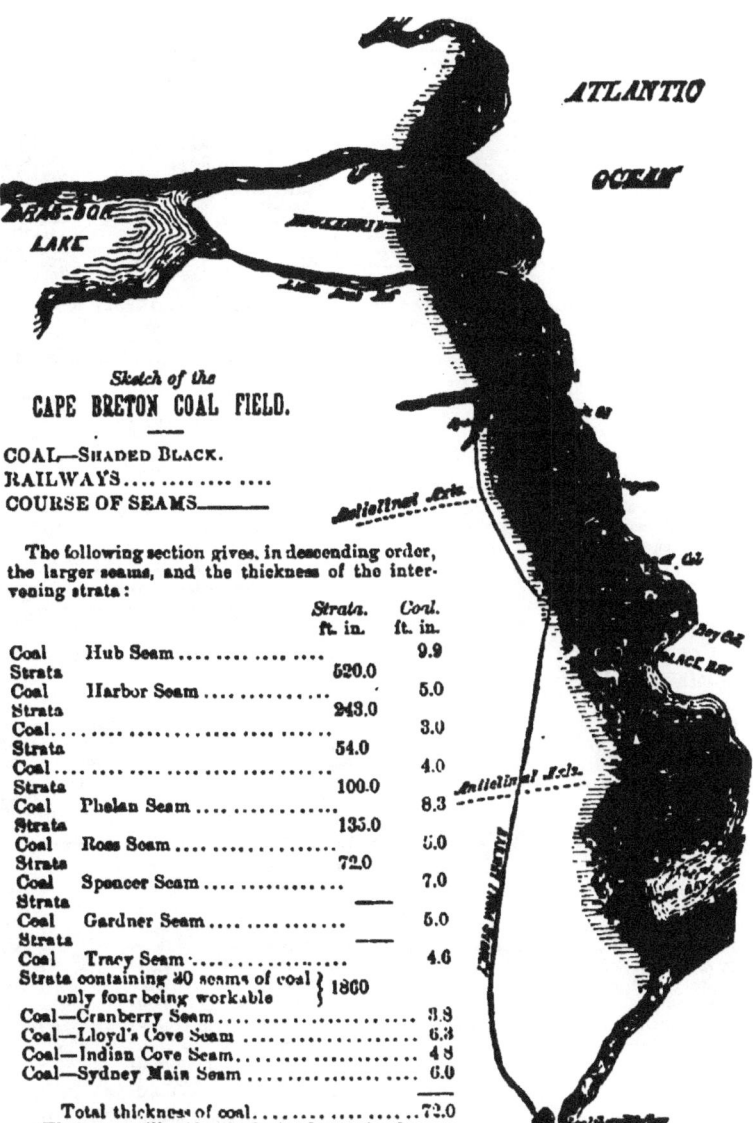

Sketch of the
CAPE BRETON COAL FIELD.

COAL—SHADED BLACK.
RAILWAYS..................
COURSE OF SEAMS_____

The following section gives, in descending order, the larger seams, and the thickness of the intervening strata:

		Strata. ft. in.	Coal. ft. in.
Coal	Hub Seam		9.9
Strata		520.0	
Coal	Harbor Seam		5.0
Strata		243.0	
Coal	....		3.0
Strata		54.0	
Coal	....		4.0
Strata		100.0	
Coal	Phalen Seam		8.3
Strata		135.0	
Coal	Ross Seam		5.0
Strata		72.0	
Coal	Spencer Seam		7.0
Strata		—	
Coal	Gardner Seam		5.0
Strata		—	
Coal	Tracy Seam		4.6
Strata containing 30 seams of coal only four being workable		1860	
Coal—Cranberry Seam			3.8
Coal—Lloyd's Cove Seam			6.3
Coal—Indian Cove Seam			4.8
Coal—Sydney Main Seam			6.0
Total thickness of coal			72.0

There are still wide blanks in the section known to contain coal seams, but we are not in possession of sufficient information to give details as to their size and position. In the Cape Breton coal measures there are over 4,500 feet of productive strata.

THE COAL TRADE.

Year.	Price per ton.	Yearly receipts.
1863	$7.40	282,774 tons.
1864	10.40	347,594 tons.
1865	9.60	465,104 tons.
1866	6.54	404,259 tons.
1867	8.10	338,452 tons.
1868	8.16	228,132 tons.
1869	7.78	257,455 tons.
1870	6.50	168,180 tons.
1871	6.54	165,431 tons.
1872	7.00	154,092 tons.
1873	7.75	232,409 tons.
1874	7.00	263,238 tons.
1875	6.00	123,114 tons.

The sales and shipments for the year 1875, were derived from the following sources :

Cumberland County	69,944 tons.
Pictou	337,102 tons.
Cape Breton	304,702 tons.
Other Counties	4,047 tons.
Total	706,795 tons.

The destination of this coal was as below :

To Nova Scotia	212,630 tons.
To New Brunswick, P. E. Island and Quebec	319,363 tons.
To Newfoundland	72,349 tons.
To United States	89,746 tons.
To West Indies	16,429 tons.
To South America	4,779 tons.
To Great Britain and East Indies	1,500 tons.

Comparing the sales of 1875 with those of the previous four years, we obtain the following table :

	1875	1874	1873	1872
Cumberland	60,944	49,599	26,345	14,153
Pictou	337,102	357,926	333,974	388,417
Cape Breton	304,702	337,016	520,199	380,373
Other counties	4,047	4,586	588	3,070
Total tons	706,795	749,127	881,106	785,814

A comparison of the *"markets"* for each year is shown below :—

Markets.	1875—Tons.	1874—Tons.	1873—Tons.
Nova Scotia	219,630	214,965	215,295
Quebec	169,754	162,169	197,059
New Brunswick	55,968	76,841	68,217
Newfoundland	62,348	55,696	55,867
P. E. Island	43,641	41,948	26,840
United States	88,746	138,395	204,760
West Indies	16,499	47,844	54,213
South America	4,779	5,077	1,883
East Indies	1,008	......	......
Great Britain	497	4,152	6,976
Total	706,795	749,127	831,106

The most serious drawback is the small coal, one seventh of all mined being what is known as slack, frequently not finding a market at any price. In 1874, the slack was 89,446 tons, and "round coal," 659,681 tons ; the introduction and use of coke ovens, will no doubt soon do away with this ; already there are a number established and in operation.

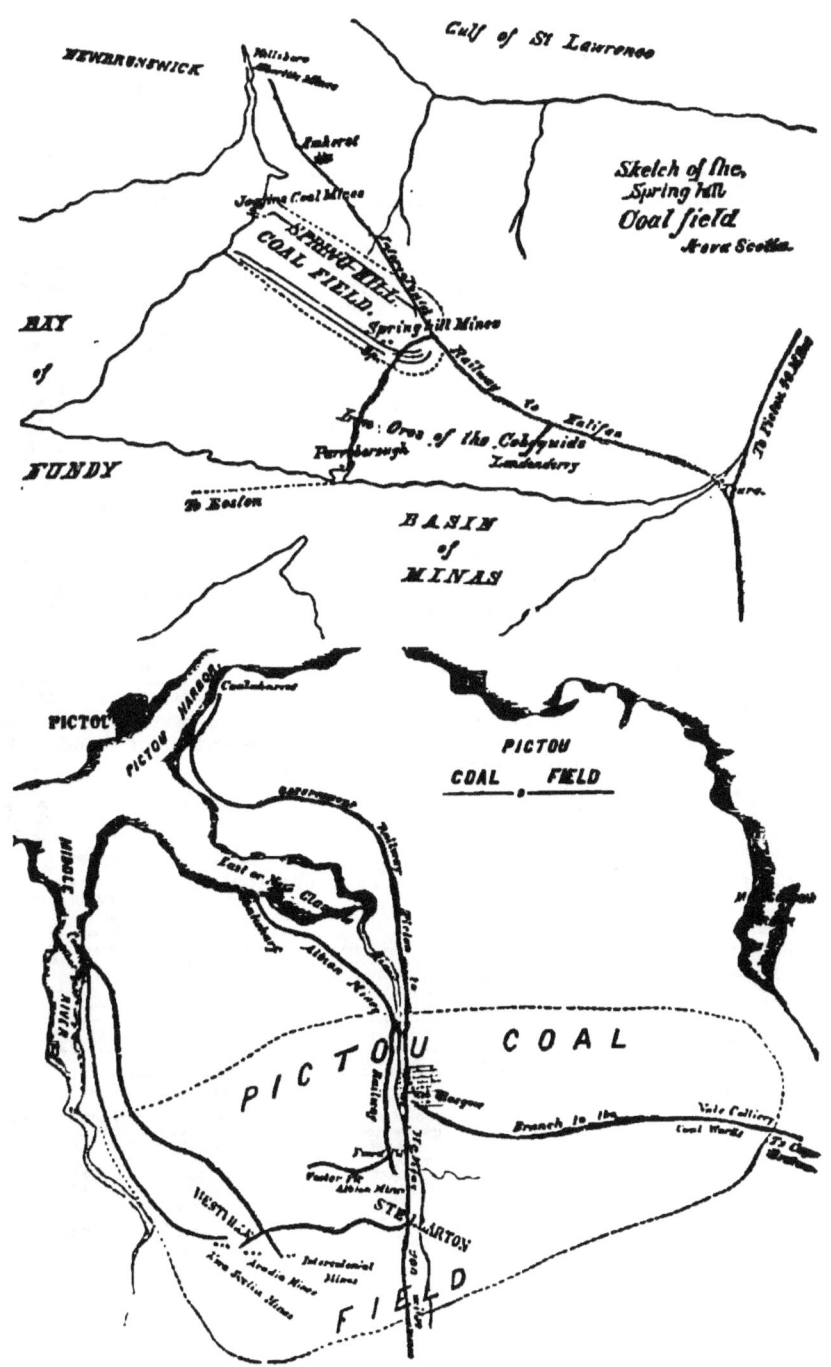

The following shows the production of each colliery for the years 1874 and 1875 :—

DISTRICT.	1875 Produce.	1874 Produce.
CUMBERLAND COUNTY.		
Cumberland	336	
Lawrence	60	27
Seaman	529	
Scotia	1,460	1,741
Joggins	11,909	16,685
Spring Hill	50,505	33,197
PICTOU COUNTY.		
Acadia	65,992	110,734
Albion, Deep	46,943	41,196
" Main	90,121	94,343
Intercolonial	72,016	68,069
Whitehall	214	90
Nova Scotia	60,824	56,963
Vale	46,547	39,099
CAPE BRETON COUNTY.		
Blockhouse	23,064	28,897
Caledonia	16,546	39,388
Collins	662	
Emery	8,356	22,137
Gardiner	10,400	20,196
Glace Bay	22,734	46,535
Gowrie	23,994	32,637
Ingraham	150	67
International	40,482	36,385
Lingan	22,505	19,697
Ontario	5,653	7,070
Reserve	9,423	28,769
Schooner Pond		1,523
South Head	1,116	
Sydney	124,199	105,437
Victoria	15,814	15,310
INVERNESS COUNTY.		
Port Hood	720	85
VICTORIA COUNTY.		
New Campbellton	4,561	5,961
Total tons of coal raised	781,165	872,730

Slack coal, is that which passes through a screen, the bars of which are not wider than three quarters of an inch. The proportion of round and slack made is shown by the following statement :

Years.	Round.	Slack.
1874	659,681	89,416
1873	810,353	70,753
1872	716,320	60,584

The following may be taken as an estimate of the items of expense in shipping a ton of coal, calculated on an annual output of 60,000 tons :

	Cents per ton.
Hewing	50
Pumping and underground work	18
Overmen and winding	10
Screening	5
Royalty	10
Railroad (five miles)	15
Shipping	5
Salaries, expenses, taxes. etc.	45
Total Canadian currency	$1.58

The ton weight designated is that of 2,240 pounds, in all cases.
An analysis of these coals gave the following results :

Mine.	Seam.	Cubic feet of gas per ton.	Candle power.	Quality of coke.	Theo. evaporative power.
Sydney.	Main Seam.	8,200	8	Good.	8.49
Lingan.	Phelan Seam.	9,700	—		9.19
Glace Bay.	Harbor Seam.	10,000	16	Good.	7.76
"	Hub Seam.	10,000	16	Fair.	8.59
Caledonia.	Phelan Seam.	9,700	16	Average.	7.83
Reserve.	Reserve Seam.	9,000	13	Average.	8.2
Block House.		10,500	14	Good.	7.69
Gowrie.	McAulay.	9,000	16	Good.	7.90

THE COAL TRADE.

GREAT BRITAIN.

The following details of the minerals produced in Great Britain are interesting:

MINERALS.	Tons raised in 1872.	Tons raised in 1873.	Tons raised in 1874.
Coal	123,497,316	127,016,747	125,043,257
Iron ore	16,494,857	15,677,409	14,544,986
Copper ore	91,983	80,195	73,521
Tin ore	14,208	14,865	14,090
Lead ore	58,968	73,800	76,301
Zinc ore	18,543	15,940	16,830
Iron pyrites	65,916	58,994	54,986
Arsenic	5,172	5,446	5,903
Bismuth	2	1	....
Cobalt	1	6 cwts	....
Manganese	7,773	8,671	5,778
Ochre, Umber, etc	8,327	6,366	7,129
Wolfram	83	50	39
Fluor spar	81	....	694
Chloride of barium	65	....	....
Barytes	9,093	10,969	14,874
Clays—fine and fire, and shale	1,200,000	1,735,000	2,436,913
Coprolites	25,000	....	140,654
Salt	1,309,495	1,735,000	2,306,567

METALS OBTAINED FROM THE ORES ENUMERATED.

	1872—tons.	1873—tons.	1874—tons.
Iron, pig	6,741,929	6,566,451	5,991,403
Tin	9,560	9,072	9,042
Copper	5,703	5,240	4,981
Lead	60,455	54,286	56,777
Zinc	5,191	4,471	4,470
Silver (ozs.)	623,920	587,707	509,277

Absolute total value of the metals and coal, with other minerals which are not smelted (except building stone, lime, slate, and common clay), produced in the United Kingdom:

	1872.	1873.	1874.
Value of the metals produced	£22,170,447	£21,409,573	£19,529,070
Value of the coal	46,311,143	47,630,787	45,849,194
Value of other minerals	1,911,926	1,681,994	2,446,049
Total	£70,198,416	£70,721,490	£67,824,313

The ton weight, in all cases, is 2240 pounds.

The following will show the amount of coal mined in the United Kingdom of Great Britain, as also the exports to foreign ports:

Year.	Tons Mined.	Tons Exported.	Year.	Tons Mined.	Tons Exported.
1854	64,600,000	4,300,000	1865	98,150,587	9,170,477
1855	61,400,000	4,940,000	1866	101,630,544	9,053,221
1856	64,600,000	5,920,000	1867	104,500,480	10,415,747
1857	65,300,000	6,600,000	1868	103,141,157	10,537,504
1858	65,000,000	6,540,000	1869	107,427,557	10,584,425
1859	71,900,000	7,080,000	1870	112,575,725	11,495,009
1860	83,700,000	7,400,000	1871	117,352,928	12,451,957
1861	85,600,000	7,905,000	1872	123,386,759	12,911,941
1862	86,500,000	7,600,000	1873	127,012,767	12,712,272
1863	88,700,000	7,501,000	1874	125,043,257	13,917,805
1864	92,757,873	8,509,908	1875	125,000,000	14,475,086

THE COAL TRADE.

The following is the disposition and uses made of the coal raised during the year 1873:

Coal exported to foreign countries	12,712,222 tons.
Coal used on railways	3,790,000 tons.
Coal used in iron manufacture	33,110,709 tons.
Coal used in smelting other metals	765,607 tons.
Coal used in mines and collieries	9,500,000 tons.
Coal used in steam navigation	3,600,000 tons.
Coal used for steam power in manufactories	27,250,000 tons.
Coal used in gas manufacture	6,500,000 tons.
Coal used in water works	650,000 tons.
Coal used in potteries, glass-works, brick, lime, cement kilns	3,450,000 tons.
Coal used in chemical works and all other sundry manufactures	3,217,229 tons.
Coal for domestic consumption	20,050,000 tons.
Making the total of	127,012,767 tons.

The production of each district for 1874 is shown in the following schedule:

Northumberland	6,463,550 tons.	Cheshire	615,105 tons.
North Durham	6,150,000 tons.	Shropshire	1,187,950 tons.
Cumberland	1,102,267 tons.	North Staffordshire	4,313,096 tons.
South Durham	17,900,250 tons.	South Staffordshire	8,389,343 tons.
Westmoreland	1,200 tons.	North East Lancashire	8,095,570 tons.
Yorkshire	14,812,515 tons.	West Lancashire	7,442,950 tons.
Derbyshire	7,150,570 tons.	Gloucester	1,147,272 tons.
Nottinghamshire	3,127,750 tons.	Somerset	609,684 tons.
Warwickshire	851,500 tons.	Monmouth	5,038,820 tons.
Leicestershire	1,100,465 tons.	North Wales	2,425,300 tons.
East Scotland	10,182,326 tons.	South Wales	10,182,326 tons.
Ireland	139,213 tons.	West Scotland	6,606,335 tons.

Total of the United Kingdom 125,067,916 tons.

The Board of Trade returns show the following shipments, from Great Britain to foreign ports, in the years named:

COUNTRIES.	1874.	1875.
Russia	883,765	884,861
Sweden and Norway	720,607	1,139,273
Denmark	662,280	760,719
Germany	2,057,020	2,154,367
Holland	447,621	455,201
France	2,370,661	2,709,494
Spain and Canaries	581,613	690,762
Italy	966,138	954,694
Turkey	311,991	241,918
Egypt	638,276	532,376
Brazil	386,357	365,172
Malta	313,022	228,981
British India	659,986	608,257
Other countries	2,726,850	2,753,659
Total	13,927,205	14,475,036
Coal for Steamers engaged in foreign trade	3,140,853	3,278,240

The receipts of coal at London for a series of years have been as below:

Year.	By Sea.	By Canal.	By Rail.	Total.
1865	3,161,683	8,532	2,733,056	5,903,271
1866	3,033,193	10,176	2,969,846	6,013,215
1867	3,016,416	9,965	3,295,652	6,322,033
1868	2,918,230	9,527	2,979,333	5,907,090
1869	2,873,688	6,941	3,341,585	6,212,214
1870	2,993,710	7,301	3,758,089	6,759,100
1871	2,762,712	6,615	4,449,141	7,218,468
1872	3,545,916	8,236	4,999,263	7,556,422
1873	2,665,630	11,195	5,147,413	7,824,288
1874	2,727,719	5,982	4,689,785	7,423,486

NEW SOUTH WALES.

The most extensively worked of the coal measures are those of Hunter River (or Newcastle,) located on the southern and western sides of the river, and include Cannel and Splint coal, and kerosene shale.

About forty miles south of Sydney commences what is known as the "Wollongong" coal measure. Outcrops have been traced for thirty miles to the southward, while inland its extent is undetermined. The seam runs from six to eight, and in one part fourteen, feet in thickness.

To the west of Sydney there is what are known as the Hartley coal measures, producing a non-caking coal, approaching a Splint and from nine to eleven feet in thickness. Communication with these mines is had by railway to Sydney. In connection with this district we may mention the Cannel coal of Petrolea Vale, a long valley running down on the northern side of Mount York. The seam is six feet in thickness, eight inches on the top and four inches at the bottom being common kerosene shale, while the remaining five feet consist of fine Cannel coal, giving an average of 150 gallons of crude oil to the ton. The seam is worked by an adit on the outcrop.

The specific gravity of the oil made from this shale is 804 at 60 degrees Fahrenheit. The "flashing point" ranges from 118 degrees to 126 degrees Fahrenheit.

W. B. Clarke, M. A., in his report on the sedimentary deposits of New South Wales, embodied in the government reports, speaks of the geological position of the shales thus :

"Recent researches have satisfied me that these only belong to the upper coal measures.

"It has unquestionably resulted from the local deposition of some resinous wood, and passes generally into ordinary coal.

"There is no anomaly in finding in one spot a mere patch in a coal seam as at Anvil Creek, on the Hunter River; or thick bedded masses, as in the coal seams of Mount York, the thickness depending on the original amount of drift timber."

W. Keene, F. G. S., government examiner of coal fields, says :

"The lower beds of the coal series of New South Wales are geologically older than any worked in Europe, while the upper beds represent the most recent of the European true carboniferous formation.

"I have examined seams more than seven hundred miles to the north of Newcastle, belonging to the same deposits we are working here (Newcastle) and we may, without boasting, claim to rank with the most extensive coal fields in the world."

It is stated that although the kerosene shale has only been worked at

Hartley and Wollongong, it may possibly be found in connection with any of the different coal seams, and as these spread over an enormous area of country, it is impossible to place any limits on the quantity of this peculiar mineral that the colony may possess.

There were twenty-eight collieries raising coal, and three getting petroleum oil, cannel coal, and shale, and the aggregate production of coal from these collieries, in 1874, was 1,298,400 tons valued at £786,152 17s.

The aggregate production of petroleum oil, cannel coal, and petroleum oil shale in 1874 was 12,100 tons, valued at £27,300.

The following is a return of the number of coal mines, and quantity and value of coal raised from the years 1864 to 1874, inclusive.

Year.	No.	Quantity. Tons—2240 lbs.	Value. £	s.	d.
1864	25	549,012½	270,171	11	0
1865	24	583,525¼	273,308	13	9
1866	25	774,238	324,049	6	7
1867	26	770,012½	342,655	7	8
1868	28	954,230¼	417,809	6	1
1869	33	919,773¼	346,145	16	5
1870	32	868.564¼	316,685	16	4
1871	27	698,784½	316,340	2	1
1872	26	1,012,426½	396,197	19	10
1873	20	1,092,861¼	665,746	17	3
1874	28	1,298,400	786,152	17	0

From these returns the Government Examiner finds that the coal trade of New South Wales is, year by year, increasing in a most satisfactory manner, and has never been in such a prosperous condition as it is at the present time. Many new companies have been formed, as well as very large areas of coal land taken up in various parts of the colony with the intention of working the coal from under it. If this rapidly increased demand for coal could have been foreseen a few years ago and the shipping facilities at Newcastle had been greater than they now are, they would have had a much larger production and demand to report, and when the extra wharves and cranes now in course of erection at the Newcastle Harbor are completed, there will be a much larger foreign demand for New South Wales coal. The agreement entered into by the associated masters and the officers and delegates of the Coal Miners' Association of the Hunter River District, by which the wages paid for hewing coal and other work usually done by the miners, the hours of labor to be observed at the different collieries, and the mode of settling any disputes that may arise in reference thereto, are to be arranged, is stated to be working well, and no doubt is entertained that it has been the means of keeping the price of coal at 14s. per ton, delivered into vessels in Newcastle Harbor.

The following detailed returns for the year 1874, are of interest in this connection, as they give the business of each district;

THE COAL TRADE. 47

NEWCASTLE DISTRICT.

Bituminous coal, used for steam, household, smelting, gas, blacksmith, and coking purposes.

Newcastle Wallsend Colliery	940,000 tons.
Australian Agricultural Company	196,404 tons.
Co-operative Colliery	149,499 tons.
Waratah Colliery	181,279 tons.
New Lambton Colliery	138,866 tons.
Lambton Colliery	127,769 tons.
Dunkenfield Colliery	2,991 tons.
Victoria Tunnel	2,146 tons.
Glen Rock Colliery	1,400 tons.
Total quantity in 1874	1,085,408 tons.

Four-mile Creek and Branxton, &c., in the Northern District.—Splint and Bituminous coals, suitable for steam, household, gas, smelting, blacksmith, and coking purposes:

Pease & Co., Four-mile Creek	11,086 tons.
Ingaree Colliery	5,666 tons.
Sunderland	1,900 tons.
Bloomfield	757 tons.
Dark Creek	150 tons.
Greta Coal and Shale Company	29,000 tons.
Anvil Creek Colliery Company	24,000 tons.
Rix's Creek, near Singleton	180 tons.
Stony Creek, near Maitland	500 tons.
Total quantity in 1874	73,708 tons.

WESTERN DISTRICT.

Lithgow Valley, Hartley, and Mudgee Road.—Splint coal used for household, steam, smelting, gas, blacksmith, and coking purposes,

Lithgow Valley Colliery	19,000 tons.
Thos. Brown, Esq., M. L. A., Eskbank Colliery	8,690 tons.
Bowenfells Colliery Company	8,500 tons.
Vale of Clywdd Company	50 tons.
Bulkeley's Coal Mine at Blackman's Flat, Mudgee Road	50 tons.
Total quantity in 1874	85,200 tons.

	Tons.	Value.
New South Wales Shale and Oil Company—petroleum oil, cannel, coal, used for oil and sold for gas purposes, 1874	9,000	£72,500

SOUTHERN OR ILLAWARRA DISTRICT.

Semi-bituminous coal, used for steam, household, smelting and blacksmith purposes.

	Tons.	Value.
Bullai Colliery	59,500	£29,268
Mount Pleasant Colliery	38.993	14,548
Osborn Wallsend Colliery	37,794	16,068
American Creek (used for oil making)	1,000	50-0
Total quantity and value in 1874	136,757	£6,884
Total quantity and value in 1873	137,090	£67,890
Decrease in 1874	773	£565
American Creek petroleum oil shale made into oil at the works	2,000	£4,570

AUSTRIA.

Austria contains such large deposits of coal wealth, that naturally she may be regarded as one of the richest coal-producing nations of Europe. Silesia, Galicia, and Bohemia are said to contain deposits of coal sufficient to supply the whole consumption of Europe for several centuries ; but this, we fear, is rather tall talk, although the coal wealth of the districts named is doubtless very considerable. It is only recently that this has been turned to profitable account. In 1818 the product on of coal in Austria and Hungary was 84,450 tons ; in 1828 it was 153,950 tons ; and in 1838, 299,100 tons. The progress made in the twenty years was not very marked, but it has since been greatly accelerated, the production having risen in 1848 to 838,000 tons ; in 1858 to 2,598,800 tons. Below will be found the details from the year 1860 up to the present time.

Years.	Pit coal.	Lignite, &c.
1860	1,739,455	1,389,023
1861	2,025,823	1,604,339
1862	2,252,951	1,811,767
1863	2,278,343	1,805,477
1864	2,203,540	1,896,158
1865	2,532,933	1,199,433
1866	2,416,783	1,952,799
1867	2,957,963	2,477,428
1868	3,334,065	2,864,962
1869	3,493,209	3,191,952
1870	3,493,250	2,960,325
1871	4,892,481	4,998,869
1872	4,713,280	5,676,672
1873	5,000,000	6,000,000

The consumption of coal during the years named has been as follows :

Years.	Tons.	Years.	Tons.
1866	4,699,737	1870	8,357,867
1867	4,707,804	1871	10,365,509
1868	6,799,899	1872	10,961,575
1869	7,529,163	1873	11,500,000
1874	12,000,000		

RUSSIA.

The chief centres of the Russian coal supply are as follows: In the south, the basin of the Lower Don, which contains 15,000 square miles of the finest Anthracite ; in the west, the governments of Kiev and Kharkoff ; and further to the north, the great central or Moscow basins, comprising the governments of Tver, Kalouga, Moscow, Raizan, Tula and Novgorod, extending northward as far as the Dwina. To these items may be added those of the Kharkoff and Ekaterinoslav beds of Anthracite, and private coal fields of the "Privis linski Krai," the districts lying to the east of the Vistula. The total area of the coal fields of the Empire of Russia is put at 30,000 square miles.

BELGIUM.

The production of coal in Belgium, and the exportations since 1836 may be observed from the following table:

Years.	Production. Tons.	Exportation. Tons.
1836	2,064,464	772,612
1846	5,087,408	1,286,923
1856	8,212,419	2,864,137
1866	12,774,662	3,977,708
1867	12,755,872	4,260,851
1868	12,396,580	3,764,592
1869	12,930,204	3,572,730
1870	13,697,118	3,196,100
1871	13,733,176	3,196,204
1872	15,658,918	4,608,100
1873	15,778,401	4,157,903
1874	14,669,079	3,956,366

The Belgian ton is 1000 kilogrammes = 2,200 pounds English.

The output is furnished by the different basins in the following proportions:

Basins.	Per cent.	Basins.	Per cent.
Mons	27.2	Liege	16.2
Charleroi	27.1	Namur	2.5
Centre	18.9		

The Province of Hainaut is the largest coal producer, furnishing 10,698,-130 tons during the year 1875. The consumption of coal in Belgium is about two tons per annum to each inhabitant. The imports of coal, mainly from England, amount to a half a million tons only, being 458,282 tons for the year 1874.

FRANCE.

There are fifty-nine small coal basins in France, but the most important are those of the Loire and St. Etienne, which are the best known, and comprise about 50,000 acres.

Probably one million tons of what is known as Anthracite, and the same quantity of soft Anthracite, are annually produced in France, the balance being Bituminous coal.

The production of coal in France, since 1787, has been as follows (tons of 2200 pounds, or ten metric quintals):

1787	211,180	1836	2,789,838	1868	13,298,876
1802	899,103	1841	3,342,508	1869	13,18,082
1811	780,878	1846	4,380,592	1870	6,850,000
1816	924,822	1852	4,516,306	1871	13,400,000
1821	1,114,446	1857	7,755,957	1872	15,899,035
1826	1,513,468	1862	10,102,116	1873	17,500,000
1831	1,728,950	1867	12,143,878	1874	17,100,000

In 1874 the Loire is set down for 3,821,200 tons; the Nord for 3,071,972 tons, and the Pas-de-Calais 2,978,600 tons.

THE COAL TRADE.

France takes annually two and a half million tons of British coal, the figures for 1875 being 2,558,678 tons.

Regarding the production and consumption of coal in France, the following may be of interest:

Years.	Production.	Consumption.
1869	13,100,100	19,424,728
1870	13,300,000	16,859,084
1871	13,00',000	18,512,248
1872	15,900,000	21,993,362
1873	17,500,000	22,700,000

The *difference between product and consumption* represents coal imported from Belgium and Great Britain.

THE GERMAN EMPIRE.

As now consolidated, Germany ranks as the largest producer of coal in Europe, and the third in the world.

The production of coal and Brown coal in Prussia for a series of years previous to the year 1871, has been as follows:

1837	1,950,915	1864	19,408,982
1857	9,841,229	1865	21,794,703
1858	10,721,823	1866	21,629,746
1860	12,347,628	1867	23,733,327
1861	14,138,046	1868	25,704,738
1862	15,576,278	1869	26,774,368
1863	16,906,707	1870	28,316,288

Since 1870, the Empire includes old Prussia, Saxony, Bavaria, and the States of the Zollverien.

The product of coal of all kinds in the whole of the German States was as follows:

Year.	Hard coal. Tons.	Brown coal. Tons.
1870	•26,397,769	•7,605,234
1871	29,373,272	8,482,837
1872	33,306,419	9,018,048
1873	36,392,279	9,252,914

The output of old Prussia is alone to be had for the year 1874; we give some interesting figures, also a comparison with 1873. There was produced in the former year 31,938,683 tons of hard coal, and 8,716,649 tons of soft or brown coal. There were 1050 mines working, at which 180,147 men were employed, supporting 307,295 persons. During 1873, 1003 mines were opened, employing 174,440 men, supporting 299,463 persons, and 32,347.409 tons of hard coal, and 7,987,333 tons of Brown coal were produced.

We have returns for the Dortmund district, which produces nearly one-half of the hard coal of the Empire, for 1875—16,805,947 tons of coal were produced, (being an increase of 9½ per cent. over product of 1874;) employ-

THE COAL TRADE.

ing 82.605 men, in 259 collieries; the value in 1875 was one-third less than in the previous year. The import and export business of the Empire was as follows:

1874—Imported........7,809.144 tons coal.	Exported..........4,299,585 tons coal.
" " ....306,432 tons coke.	" ....146,035 tons coke.
1873—Imported..........1,456,497 tons coal.	Exported..........4,010,406 tons coal.
" " ....548,553 tons coke.	" ....42,468 tons coke.

The value of the imports in 1873 was eighteen million thalers, while the exports were valued at thirty-three million thalers.

It is usual to count twenty German centners as one ton, and as they are 113.38 pounds English, the tons mentioned above are 2,267 pounds, or 27 pounds more than our gross tons.

WEST VIRGINIA.

The coal measures of West Virginia underlay nearly sixteen thousand square miles of territory, of which, what is known is the Kanawha and New River Valleys hold eight thousand. Three varieties of coal occur: cannel, splint, and bituminous. Of the bituminous there are seams of different degrees of hardness and texture, from the friable coking coal, similar to the best of the Newcastle (England) coals, to the harder splint coals, with regular cleavage, similar to the Youghiogheny coals so largely in demand in our Western and Southern cities; of so compact a nature that it can be used in an iron blast furnace in its raw state.

The bituminous coals are excellent steam raising fuels, and have been used in steamers, railways, and under stationary engines with good results. The gas coal seam is identical with the Kittaning coal bed, mined on the Allegheny river, in Pennsylvania, and has been used in the eastern and western markets with most satisfactory results.

On approaching from the eastward, the bituminous coal seams of West Virginia are first found in the tops of the mountain ranges overlooking New river, in Summers and Raleigh counties, embracing only the lowest seams of what are known as the lower coal measures. The Big Sewell mountain a prominent elevation in West Virginia, towering some 2,800 feet above sea level, and 1,500 feet above New river, forms the south eastern edge of the "Upper Ohio coal basin." All the territory drained by the Kanawha and its tributaries, between the Falls of the Kanawha and Campbell's creek, contains the seams of coal within workable reach, above water level, or by shafts at no great depth. It can be mined very cheaply; and the quantity available is vast beyond conception. The top seam of the lower coal measures disappears beneath the Kanawha, at its confluence with the Elk river, at Charleston; while some of the coal seams reappear up the valleys formed by the Elk and Coal Rivers. Cabin creek, Elk river, and Coal river are three considerable tributaries to the Kanawha, penetrating the country for long distances, and bringing into convenient working position thousands of acres of valuable coal land.

At Quinnimont, on the line of the Chesapeake and Ohio Railroad, 295 miles west of Richmond, are the works of the New River Car Co. Analysis made by J. B. Britton, gave the following results:

Coal		Coke run of mines.	Coke from slack.
Fixed Carbon............75.89	Carbon............93.85	91.73
Volatile Matter............19.19	Ash............ 5.94	5.09
Ash............ 4.93	Sulphur............ 0.51	0.48
Moisture............ 0.74	Water............ —	2.71

This company is mining a vein about 3¼ feet bituminous coal, using the

the coke in their blast furnace, for the manufacture of car wheels. The coke is fully equal to the famous Connellsville, of Pennsylvania.

At Nuttallburg, 316 miles west from Richmond, John Nuttall, Esq., is mining a Bituminous coal from the lower coal measures; the vein is 3½ feet thick far above water level. The coal finds a market east for steam purposes. The Old Dominion Steamship Co., has been using this coal with satisfaction. The slack coal is made into coke, for the manufacture of which he is now erecting ovens. The coke has been used for iron smelting and for foundries with great success, being pronounced by those who have tried it, equal to the best Connellsville coke.

At Hawk's Nest, 325 miles west from Richmond, are the works of the Gauley-Kanawha Co , an English concern. Their coal was analyzed at the School of Mines, in London, with the following result: Carbon, 83.31; hydrogen, 5.54; oxygen and nitrogen, 6.86; sulphur, 0.74; ash, 2.15; water, 1.40.

At Cannelton, 344 miles west from Richmond, the Cannelton company are working the coal, which is so well known in the eastern and western markets. At this point there are the following seams of coal: The first, known as the "Smithers Creek," 4 feet 9 inches in thickness (two benches of coal separated by four inches of slate.) Next above is the gas coal, of 6 feet 8 inches, made up of three benches; the coal is a first class gas coal. Above this is a seam of coal 5 feet in thickness, of semi-bituminous quality. Above this is the "Stockton" seam of coal, 5 feet 4 inches in thickness, averaging 3½ feet of cannel, and 1 foot 10 inches of splint coal. Next above is a seam of "Splint" coal, 8 feet in thickness, 6 feet of which is a solid mass, and an excellent coal for smelting purposes. We give an analysis of the Cannelton, made by the Manhattan Gas Light Co., of New York: Volatile matter, 58.0; fixed carbon, 23.5; ash, 18.5. At standard (10,000 cubic feet) it gave an illuminating power of 64.54 candles, or 12,025 cubic feet of 45.60 candles. Weight of 32 bushels of coke, 1320 pounds.

In the vicinity of Coalburg (Brownstown) 354 miles west from Richmond, are several operations, working coal which is highly appreciated by ironmasters as an excellent fuel, in its raw state, in the reduction of iron ores, and also for steam and domestic purposes in the Ohio river markets. Analyses made of the bituminous coal from this locality show: Fixed carbon, 56.0 to 62.6; volatile matter, 40.5 to 33.3; ash, 1.5 to 1.8; water, 2.0 to 2.5.

At Peytons, in Boone county, are the mines of the Peytona Cannel Coal Co., located on Coal river, about thirty-five miles from its junction with the Great Kanawha river, 380 miles west from Richmond. The coal is transported by slackwater navigation to the mouth of Coal river, where a connection is made with the C. & O. R. R. The great part of the product of

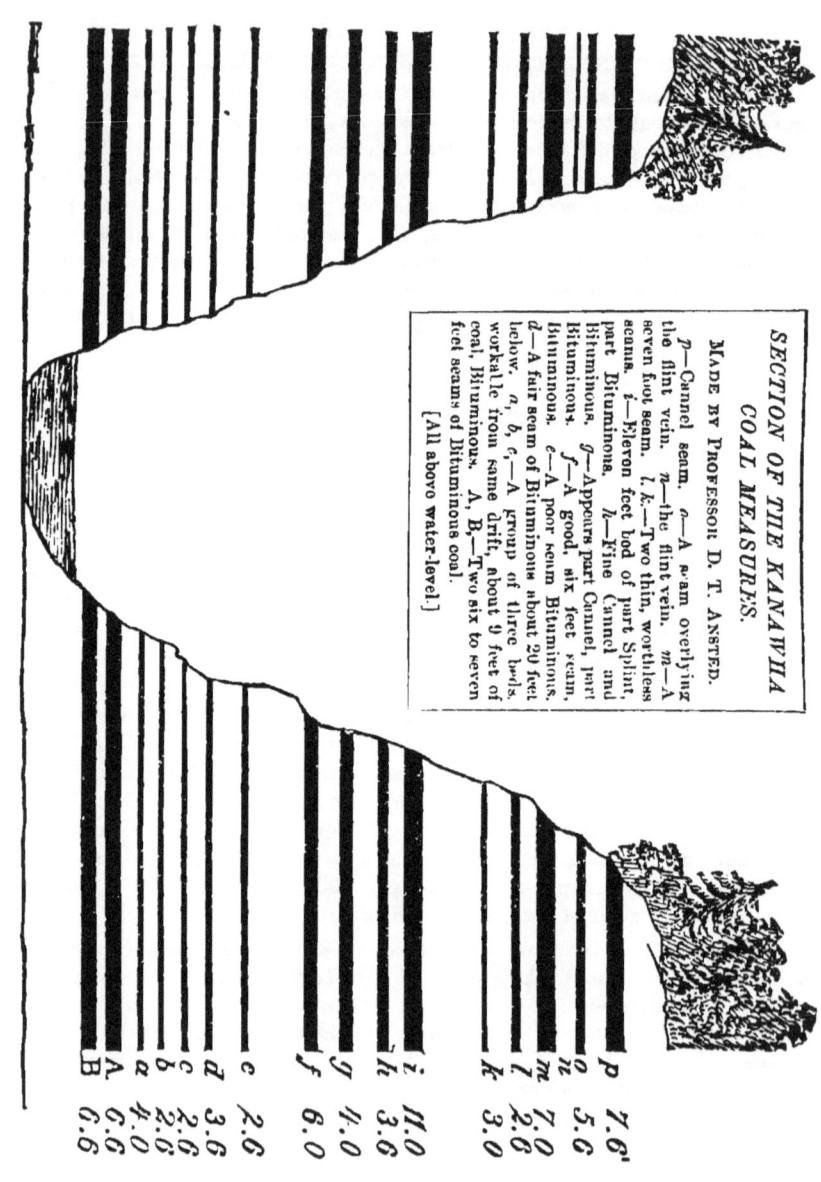

SECTION OF THE KANAWHA COAL MEASURES.

MADE BY PROFESSOR D. T. ANSTED.

p—Cannel seam. *o*—A seam overlying the flint vein. *n*—the flint vein. *m*—A seven foot seam. *l*, *k*.—Two thin, worthless seams. *i*—Eleven feet bed of part Splint, part Bituminous. *h*—Fine Cannel and bituminous. *g*—Appears part Cannel, part Bituminous. *f*—A good, six feet seam, Bituminous. *e*—A poor seam Bituminous. *d*—A fair seam of Bituminous about 20 feet below. *a*, *b*, *c*,—A group of three beds, workable from same drift, about 9 feet of coal, Bituminous. A, B.—Two six to seven feet seams of Bituminous coal.

[All above water-level.]

p 7.6′
o 5.6
n 7.0
m 2.6
l 3.0
k
i 11.0
h 3.6
g 4.0
f 6.0
e 2.6
d 3.6
c 2.6
b 4.0
a 6.6
A 6.6
B

the mines has been forwarded westward by the Kanawha and Ohio rivers to Cincinnati, and other important places bordering the rivers. The coal is also sold in the Eastern markets, where it is esteemed both for gas purposes and fuel. We give place to an analysis of this coal made by the Manhattan Company. Volatile matter, 46.0 ; fixed carbon, 44.0 ; ash, 13.0. At 10,000 feet per ton, standard yield, the illuminating power is 43.12 candles, or 13,200 cubic feet of 32.66 candles. Weight of coke, 32 bushels=1380 pounds.

In regard to an outlet from this region, we have the Chesapeake and Ohio Railway eastward, the building of which has done so much to open up this district. Their charges for carrying coal are extremely liberal, when we consider that it is comparatively a new road, and has many obstacles to surmount from errors in the original location of the line ; a more decided move seems to have been inaugurated this year, looking to the development of the coal trade, and in time it is destined to carry considerable quantities of coal.

The Government improvements of the navigation of the Kanawha river, by dams and locks, will tend to develop the resources of this most wonderful region, and, in a few years, it will not be surprising to find this the iron making district of America.

The total coal product of West Virginia may safely be estimated at 600,000 tons per annum.

MISSOURI.
[From the report of G. C. Brodhead, State Geologist for 1874.]

The coal measures of Missouri comprise an area of about 22,995 square miles, including 160 square miles in St. Louis county, 80 in St. Charles, and a few outliers in Lincoln and Warren ; the remainder in northwest and western Missouri. This includes 8,406 square miles of upper or barren measures, about 2,000 square miles of exposed middle, and 12,420 of lower measures.

The boundary between the middle and lower coal is not well defined, but is limited by a thick-bedded, coarse, micaceous sandstone, sometimes of no great extent, at other times of great thickness. We suppose it to enter the State in the west part of Bates county, and to pass thence via Butler to Chilhomeo in Johnson county ; thence northwardly four miles west of Warrensburgh to four miles east of (?) Aullville, Lafayette county ; thence, irregularly meandering through Lafayette county, crossing the Missouri river, passing to ten miles east of Carrollton, Carroll county ; thence to the southeast corner of Livingston county, from which point it bears northeast to the center of Linn county, and thence, northward. The southern and eastern boundary of the lower coal measures is as follows: (through Barton, Bates, Vernon and St. Clair, the boundary has not yet been well defined;) entering the State in Barton, it passes northeast through the eastern part of Vernon; it enters St. Clair about one half way up, on its western line, thence, meanders eastward to a point a few miles north of Osceola; thence, northward to within eight miles of Clinton, Henry county, thence northeast to the east line of Henry county; thence northwardly, with occasional variations of sandstones as much as eight miles east to Brownsville, Saline county; thence north-eastward to Marshall and thence to Miami. On the north side of the river it passes eastward, from a point opposite Arrow Rock, to the east line of Howard county; and thence, in a meandering course via Columbia, Boone county, New Bloomfield and Fulton, Callaway county, to the northeast corner of Callaway; thence, northeastwardly to a point three miles west of the northeast corner of Montgomery county; thence northwest to near the mouth of Lick creek, Ralls county: thence, southwest to Mexico, Audrain county; from thence, to the northwest corner of Monroe county, thence, irregularly trending northward to the northwest corner of Knox county; thence, to a point on the north line of Lewis county, about 12 miles west of the Mississippi river; thence northwardly to the Des Moines river, on the north line of the State of Missouri. East of this, are small outliers in Montgomery, Warren, Lincoln and St. Louis counties, and perhaps others in southwest Missouri.

The aggregate thickness of the upper coal measures is 1,317 feet, including only about 4 feet of coal, of which there are two seams of one foot in thickness; the others are very thin seams or mere streaks. The middle coal measures include a total thickness of about 324 feet, in which are embraced about 7 feet of coal, including two workable seams of 21 and 24 inches; one other of one foot, that is worked under favorable circumstances, and six seams too thin to work. The lower measures include from 250 to 300 feet, embracing about five workable seams of coal, varying in thickness from 1½ to 4½ feet, and thin seams varying from 6 to 11 inches, and several minor seams and streaks; in all 13 feet 6 inches of coal. We therefore have in Missouri nearly 1,900 feet of coal measures with a total aggregate of 24 feet 6 inches of coal. The thinner seams of coal are not often mined, except in localities remote from railroad transportation. The coal from thicker seams (those from 1½ to 2 and 4 feet) is generally sold at 10 cents per bushel at the mines. The thin seam, 10 to 14 inches on Nodaway river, is sold at over 20 cents per bushel at the mines. The reason of this is the difficulty of mining (there being so much superfluous material to be removed) and the remoteness of other coals. Miners seem to prefer to work a bed of 2 to 2½ feet in thickness. We would consider all beds over

18 inches thick as workable coals. The estimated area, where such may be reached within 200 feet from the surface, is about 7,000 square miles. The coal is bituminous, and the product may be safely estimated at 800,000 tons.

The following is a condensed vertical section of the coal measures:

No.	Locality.
1—839 feet, including 230 feet above the connected section..................	
2—12 inches coal..................	Holt, west part of Nodaway and northwardly; also White Cloud, Kansas.
3—392 feet..................	
4—12 inches coal..................	Andrew, Buchanan, De Kalb, Gentry and Platte
5—207 feet..................	
6—10 inches coal..................	Platte county.
7—319 feet to base of upper coal measures.........	
8—3 inches coal at top of middle coal measures....	Pleasant Hill, Missouri City and Princeton Mercer County.
9—164 feet..................	
10—1 foot coal..................	Cass, Johnson, Lafayette and Livingston, also Grundy.
11—70 feet..................	
12—22 feet (Lexington coal)..................	Lafayette, Johnson and Ray.
13—36 feet..................	
14—7 inches coal..................	Lafayette and Ray.
15—14 feet..................	
16—21 inches coal..................	Lafayette, Johnson, Carroll and Livingston.
17.—5) to 90 feet..................	
18—1½ feet (Warrensburgh coal)..................	Johnson, Henry and Chariton.
19—52 feet..................	
20—7 inches coal..................	Johnson.
21—19 feet..................	
22—1 foot 8 inches coal..................	Johnson.
23—18 feet..................	
24—9 inches coal..................	Johnson.
25—4 feet..................	
26—2 feet coal..................	Henry.
27.—46 feet..................	
28—2½ feet to 4 feet 5 inches coal..................	Randolph, Boone, Callaway, Johnson, Henry, Vernon, Bates, Adair, Sullivan, Putnam, Audrain and Macon.
29—11 feet..................	Macon.
30—11 inches coal..................	Macon, Henry and Johnson.
31—About 13 feet..................	
32—2 feet coal; 10 inches of clay near base........	Ralls, Audrain, St. Louis, St. Charles and Montgomery, Henry and Johnson.

OHIO.

The coal measures within this State occupy a space of about 180 miles in length by 80 in breadth at the widest part, with an area of about 10,000 square miles, extending along the Ohio river from Trumbull county, on the north, to near the mouth of the Scioto, on the south. The counties wholly underlain with coal are Mahoning, Columbiana, Stark, Holmes, Tuscarawas, Carroll, Jefferson, Harrison, Belmont, Guernsey, Coshocton, Muskingum,

Perry, Noble, Morgan, Monroe, Washington, Athens, Miegs, Galla, Lawrence, and nearly all of Jackson. The counties of which the eastern or southeastern parts only are underlain with coal are Trumbull, Summit, Medina, Wayne, Licking, Fairfield, Hocking, Vinton, and Scioto. There are small detached basins in Wayne, Ashland, Richland. and Knox counties. The boundary on the east is the State line, the same field extending eastward over all western Pennsylvania.

Prof. J. S. Newberry, divides the coals of Ohio into three classes—first, the dry, open-burning or furnace coals; second, cementing or coking coals; third, cannel coals, the first, which is popularly known as block coal, includes those that do not coke and adhere in the furnace, and are such as may be used in the raw state for the manufacture of iron. The second, embracing by far the greater portion, are of the ordinary coking, bituminous kinds, which to a greater or less degree melt and agglutinate by heat. The third variety consists of the cannel coals, which resemble a dark shale, highly impregnated with bitumen, and burns with a bright flame, but does not agglutinate.

The chief mining regions of Ohio are the Mahoning Valley, the Tuscarawas Valley, the Hocking Valley, including the Straitsville and Shawnee mines, the Salineville region, the Pomeroy region, the Bellaire region, the Steubenville region, the Jackson region, the Cambridge region, the Coshocton region, the Leetonia region, and the Ironton region.

The mines of Mahoning Valley, the Tuscarawas Valley, and the Jackson region are all opened on the lower coal of the measures, called Briar Hill coal, Block coal, furnace coal, etc. It is usually about four feet thick. The mines of Hocking region, Steubenville, part of Salineville, Cambridge, are opened on No. 6, which ranges from 4 to 13 feet of thickness and is open burning in quality also. The others are worked in each of the different beds, of which there are ten altogether of minable thickness.

The chemical analysis of the Ohio coals shows that the relative amount of moisture varies from 1.10 per cent. to something over 9.10 per cent. The amount of volatile matter varies from 28 per cent to something over 40 per cent. Fixed carbon varied from 34.10 (in the upper coal from Holmes county) to 65.90 (in the coal from Steubenville shaft.) The ash found in eleven Ohio cannel coals was 12.827 per cent. The average proportion of sulphur was 1.551 per cent, that from the lower half of the State being 1.229 per cent. and that of the coal from the upper half 1.836 per cent.

Coal was discovered in Tallmadge, a mile west of the Centre, as early as 1816. It was visible in a small ravine, where for many years blacksmiths from the adjacent country came and dug it from an open pit. At that time no other coal was known in Northern Ohio. As early as 1755, mineral coal had been discovered near Bolivar, in Tuscarawas county, by its being seen on fire, but it was not dug or mined for use as fuel, in this part of the State, prior to 1810. The seam was 4 feet thick, and was regularly mined in 1820.

The Perry county coal field is now, dating back only to 1870; yet the seven mines at Straitsville take out as much coal daily, as the whole of Hickory township combined. This coal is of about the same character as the block coal of Mercer, Trumbull, Mahoning and other adjoining counties, is 11 feet thick, although there are two other veins, one under and one above the "great vein," aggregating another 11 feet, making in all 22 feet of coal in three veins, in the same hill, all above the water level.

Cleveland and Erie have hitherto had a monopoly of the trade by lake, but it will soon embrace several other lake towns. Toledo, Sandusky, Black River, Fairport, and Ashtabula have roads leading to the mines, the principal object of which is to bring out coal.

An analysis of the block coals of the Mahoning Valley gave the following results:

	I.	II.	III.
Specific Gravity	1.251	1.260	1.328
Water	3.60	2.47	3.30
Volatile Matter	32.54	31.82	29.70
Fixed Carbon	62.68	64.26	60.40
Ash	1.16	1.45	6.60
	100.—	100.—	100.—

No. 1—Sample of Briar Hill, from Chestnut Ridge.
No. 2—From Vratch's mine, Youngstown.
No. 3—From Walworth's mine, Mahoning County.

Mr. Andrew Roy, State Inspector of Mines, gives the production of coal in this State as below:

| 1872 | 5,815,794 tons. | 1874 | 3,207,583 tons. |
| 1873 | 5,430,094 tons. | 1875 | 4,846 250 tons. |

The number of persons employed in coal mining in this State in 1875 was 12,096 underground, and 1,373 on the surface. The business of that year was furnished by the various counties to the following extent:

County.	Production.	County.	Production.
Athens	829,508 tons.	Muskingum	109,490 tons.
Belmont	213,506 tons.	Mahoning	871,669 tons.
Carroll	60,000 tons.	Meigs	345,500 tons.
Columbia	332,416 tons.	Noble	4,000 tons.
Coshocton	90,649 tons.	Perry	502,100 tons.
Guernsey	183,427 tons.	Stark	408,180 tons.
Gallia	5,490 tons.	Tuscarawas	107,000 tons.
Hocking	170,080 tons.	Summit	274 876 tons.
Holmes	14,000 tons.	Trumbull	749,030 tons.
Harrison	5,300 tons.	Vinton	54,856 tons.
Jefferson	193,985 tons.	Wayne	60,291 tons.
Lawrence	122,494 tons.	Washington	12,425 tons.
Medina	80,000 tons.	Small mines	80,000 tons.

ARKANSAS.

The coal field of Arkansas has an area of 12,000 square miles, in twelve counties. The coal found is semi-bituminous or semi-anthracite. A bed of semi-bituminous coal nine feet thick is reported in Sebastian County. The Spadra semi-anthracite is the only coal that is known in market to any extent, and an account of its location, etc., will prove interesting. "This name is given to a deposit of semi-anthracite coal, three feet thick, found at Spadra, in Johnson County, 105 miles from Little Rock, now being worked by the Spadra Coal and Iron Company. It lies almost horizontal, with a slight dip to the north. It crops out on the river bank, and is traceable along the river front. On digging anywhere, the same vein, from $3\frac{1}{4}$ to 4 feet thick, is invariably struck within 55 feet of the level of the river front. The product is about 5,000 tons. The existence of a second vein, which is, as near as can be ascertained, about 30 feet below the one working now, is a matter of development. The coal can be placed at Little Rock at $3.25 a ton; at the mouth of the Arkansas River, $3.75 a ton; at New Orleans for $5 a ton; at St. Louis, $6.75 per ton."

The only coal to compete with on the lower Mississippi, from the mouth of the Arkansas to New Orleans, 600 miles—which section of country consumes about one million of tons per annum—is the Bituminous coal, principally furnished by Pittsburgh.

Professor Owen gives an analysis of the coal in the First Geological Report on Arkansas, page 130. It was also analysed by Mr. I. A. Liebig, and by L. C. Bierwirth, with the following results:

	OWEN.	LIEBIG.	BIERWIRTH.
Moisture	0.5	1.524	0.680
Volatile and combustible gases	7.9	7.527	10.521
Fixed carbon	85.6	85.081	83.719
Ashes	6.0	5.468	5,080
Total	100.	100.	100.
Specific gravity	1.335	1.8409	1.3112

In addition there is the Ouita Coal Co., producing an excellent variety of semi-anthracite, to the extent of seven thousand tons a year; the mines are seventy-two miles from Little Rock; the vein is 32 inches thick. Analysis gave 80.46 fixed carbon; 12.66 volatile matter; ash, 5.11; water, 1.77; color of ash, light brown. One or two other small mines producing less than one thousand tods annually.

ILLINOIS.

The valuable features of the coal found in this State are, that there is plenty of it, that it is very widely distributed over the State, and readily accessible. Although it is generally necessary to mine it by means of shafts, the coal is reached at so reasonable a depth from the surface that its mining is done without unusual expense; the number of railroads traversing all parts of this State, with good level grades and without curves, furnish an abundance of cheap transportation, and there is a large market for the coal that is produced.

The valuable iron-smelting Big Muddy coal, found in the southern part of the State, and extensively used at St. Louis, as well as some of a fair quality in other localities, would lead us to the hope of yet finding coal of a better quality than much of that which is now mined.

The United States census of 1870 reports the production of coal in Illinois at 2,629,563 tons. To those accustomed to the large production of Eastern mines near our seaboard these figures may appear small, but it should be considered that the coal business in the West is yet in its infancy. In La Sal'e County there are three seams of coal, the upper four and a half to five feet thick, the middle usually six feet, and the lower four feet. The most popular in the market is the middle, as it makes a dense fire, and is largely used for steam and domestic uses. In 1870 the product was 173,864 tons, according to the census reports, and this has probably been doubled by this time. What is known as Wilmington coal is found in Will and Livingston Counties, the seam averaging three feet in thickness. The amount in 1875 was 512,800 tons. It makes a good steam coal, and is much liked for locomotive use. This district furnishes the principal supply of soft coal used in Chicago The mining is carried on principally by three companies. The Wilmington and Vermilion Co. has a daily capacity of 1800 tons. The Star Company has a capacity of 1000 tons a day; produced 117.680 tons in 1875. The Wilmington Coal and Manufacturing Company has a producing capacity of over 500 tons daily. The Eureka Coal Co., mined 131,615 tons in 1875 ; the C. W. & W. Coal Co., 225,879 tons. The opening of the Chicago and Illinois River Railroad, which pierces the heart of this coal district thus furnishes Chicago with a supply of cheap and valuable fuel.

St. Louis, Missouri, obtains a large supply of Bituminous coal from the Belleville district, in St. Clair County, Illinois. This county contains 450 square miles of coal, and the last census returns show a production in this county of 793,810 tons. The principal seam worked is from five to seven feet in thickness, and is economically mined. Analysis of this coal shows: Water, 6; volatile matter, 33.8; fixed carbon, 55.2; ash, 5.

In Vermilion County the seam is six feet thick, furnishing a good fat, soft caking coal. The vein is from seventy to one hundred feet below the surface, and is very thick and of excellent quality. Mining was begun in 1867. The annual product is 250,000 tons.

The production of coal in the entire State in 1875 is estimated at 3,750,000 tons.

INTERESTING FACTS AND FIGURES.

WEIGHT OR MEASURE.

The Constitution of the United States provides for a "standard of weights and measures," but at present there is not a national observance of this enactment. We have bushels, boxes, hogsheads, tons 2,000 lbs., and 2,240 lbs., oftentimes two or more systems in one State, and occasionally in the same region. We propose that all coal be mined, carried and sold at 2,000 lbs. to the ton, wholesale and retail. It will then be possible to calculate production, compare prices and in fact, set the whole trade on a substantial foundation, which is impossible under the present disorganized and sectional system of measurement. Reader, will you please give this matter your earnest attention?

LARGE MINE VENTILATOR.

The largest mine ventilator in the world is a Guibal fan, 45 feet in diameter, and 12 feet face, at the Usworth colliery, near Newcastle-on-Tyne, England. This fan runs about forty-five revolutions per minute, and is said to circulate 200,000 to 250,000 cubic feet of air per minute. It is driven by two first motion engines, 36 inch diameter cylinders, 3 feet stroke. The upcast shaft is 10 feet diameter, and 600 feet deep. The workings in three seams are ventilated through it. The output of the Usworth Colliery is about 1,500 tons per day. The mines are very extensive. All the underground haulage is performed by machinery; two of the three seams are worked on the bord and pillar system; the other is worked on the longwall plan.

COAL TRADE ON LAKE ERIE.

The first time that Bituminous coal appears as an article of commerce on the Lake was in the year 1829, when the northern division of the Ohio canal was opened from Akron, Ohio, on the edge of the Ohio coal field. Up to 1854 it was brought by this means to Cleveland, In that year the Cleveland and Pittsburgh and the Cleveland and Mahoning roads penetrated the coal fields, and gave another outlet. The Bituminous coal from Mercer County, Pennsylvania, is received and shipped at Erie, Pennsylvania. These two ports transact about all the Bituminous coal business of Pennsylvania and Ohio on the lakes.

ASPHALTUM DEPOSITS.

Asphalt is a natural mineral bitumen, and is composed of asphaltene and petrolene. In nature it is found combined with carbonate of lime and other mineral substances. It fuses only at about 400 degrees Farenheit, and maintains its hardness under a constant heat of 150 degrees Farenheit. This substance was formerly obtained almost solely from the neighborhood of the Dead Sea, but within five years, the great lake of asphalt in the island of Trinidad has been used as a source of supply both for the United States and Europe. This lake is one of the most remarkable natural curiosities in the world, and its existence has never been satisfactorily explained. It is circular in shape, and covers about 114 acres. Its depth is unknown, although it is estimated to be 800 feet. The asphaltum constantly bubbles up in the centre, and flows outward. On the outer edges it hardens, and will sustain carts and teams 200 or 300 feet from the shore. It is cut out in blocks, refined by heat, and finds its way to market molded into barrels For paving city streets, asphalt is fast coming into general use in Europe. In Paris, all the boulevards and other principal streets are paved with it, and in London no other material is now allowed to be used for laying pavements.

COAL IN RHODE ISLAND.

The Mount Hope coal mine, in Portsmouth, Rhode Island, contains the hardest Anthracite in this country, if not in the world. It is much lighter colored than the ordinary Anthracite, and in many places it strongly resembles plumbago. The mine yields about 15,000 tons a year, and it is pretty good fuel, though when the beds were opened, many years ago, it was thought to be next to worthless. It sells for from $2 50 to $4 50 a ton at the mine. Large quantities of this coal are consumed at the mine, in smelting copper from Chili.

COAL IN TEXAS.

The coal-bearing rocks of Texas occupy an area of not less than six thousand miles, embracing the counties of Jack, Young, Palo, Pinto, Eastland, Brown, Comanche, Callahan, Coleman, and extending to the territory of Bexar. The rocks contain the characteristics belonging to the coal measures of Missouri and other Western States. In general appearance this coal resembles that of Belleville, Illinois. The analysis gives:—Fixed Carbon, 56 per cent.; Volatile Matter, 34 per cent.; Ashes, 8 per cent. It cokes with a great flame, without changing its form. Anthracites, lighter and more brittle than those of Pennsylvania, have been found in various parts of the State. Lignites, and other coals of more recent origin, occupy an area of ten thousand square miles.

UNDERGROUND TEMPERATURE.

Regarding underground temperatures, a very valuable set of observations has been received from a mine, 1,900 feet deep, in Prague, Bohemia. The depths, and corresponding temperatures are as follows:

Depth in feet.	Degrees Fahrenheit.	Depth in feet.	Degrees Fahrenheit.
68	47.9	1290	55.3
230	46.8	1414	59.4
461	50.7	1668	61.4
980	57.8	1900	64.1

DEEPEST COAL PIT.

The deepest pit in the world is said to be at Chatelineau, three miles from Charleroi, Belgium. It is 2608 feet deep from the surface, and it was intended to sink another shaft in a tunnel from the bottom of the first shaft, a further depth of 492 feet, making a total depth of 3314 feet. The deepest coal shaft in England is the Dunkenfield, 2,000 feet, took ten years time to sink, cost $900,000, and this to reach a bed of coal only 4 ft. 8½ inches thick.

DISTANCES TO MARKET.

The following are the distances from a portion of the American coal fields, to the different tidewater markets:

FROM	BY	MILES.
Pottsville to New York	Canal	276
Pottsville to New York	Rail and Water	196
Pottsville to Philadelphia	Canal	106
Pottsville to Philadelphia	Rail	98
Mauch Chunk to New York	Lehigh Canal	173
Mauch Chunk to New York	Morris Canal	147
Mauch Chunk to New York	Rail	136
Mauch Chunk to Philadelphia	Canal	134
Mauch Chunk to Philadelphia	Rail	80
Carbondale to New York	Rail and Canal	208
Scranton to New York	Rail	143
Wilkesbarre to New York	Rail	192
Wilkesbarre to Philadelphia	Rail and Canal	168
Wilkesbarre to Mauch Chunk	Rail	85
Wilkesbarre to Baltimore	Rail and Canal	260
Wilkesbarre to Baltimore	Canal	246
Shamokin to Baltimore	Rail and Canal	260
Shamokin to Baltimore	N. Cent. R. R.	158
Cumberland to Baltimore	Rail	178
Cumberland to Georgetown	Canal	184
Cumberland to Alexandria	Canal	191
Broad Top to Philadelphia	Rail	243
Clearfield to Philadelphia	Rail	240
Westmoreland to Philadelphia	Rail	339
Blossburg to New York	Rail	300
Kanawha to Richmond	Rail	395

COAL IN MICHIGAN.

The only coal that has been used at all successfully, that is mined in this State, is found in Jackson County. The business is very small, amounting to not over 20,000 tons annually. An analysis gives it:—Carbon, 45; Volatile Matter, 30; Ash, 2; Sulphur, 2; Water, 2. This great State is therefore supplied with fuel by our Pennsylvania and Ohio coal mines.

VOLUME OF GAS OBTAINED FROM A TON OF COAL.

	CUBIC FEET.	SPECIFIC GRAVITY.
Boghead Cannel	13,934	.42
Wigan Cannel	15,426	.73
Cannel	15,000	.59
Cape Breton	9,500	—
Cumberland	10,000	—
English, *mean*	11,000	.24
Newcastle	10,000	.05
Kilkenny	12,500	.04
Oil and Grease	23,000	.67
Pictou and Sydney	8,000	—
Pine Wood	11,000	.66
Pittsburgh Coal	9,520	—
Resin	15,600	.66
Scotch Coal	15,000	.56
Virginia Coal	8,963	—
Wallsend	12,000	.42

CUBIC CONTENTS OF A TON.

Few persons have any idea as to the amount of coal that can be stowed in a given space; we therefore give an example of the manner in which it may be figured up. A shed or room, 15 feet high, 18 feet wide, and 30 feet long, will hold 200 tons of Anthracite coal, and perhaps ten tons less of Cumberland. Thus 15×18×30 = 5100, divided by 4½, average cubic contents of a ton of Anthracite — 202½.

The average number of cubic feet required to stow a ton of coal is as follows:

BITUMINOUS.

Cumberland, maximum	42.3
do. minimum	41.2
Duffryn, (Welsh)	42,99
Cannel, (Lancashire)	46.87
Blossburg, Pa	42.2
Hartley, Newcastle	44.
Pictou, Nova Scotia	45.
Pittsburgh, Pa	47.06
Sydney, Cape Breton	47.02
Clover Hill, Va	49.02
Cannelton, Indiana	47.
Scotch	43.03
Richmond, Va., (Midlothian)	41.04

ANTHRACITE.

Peach Mountain	41.06
Forest Improvement	41.07
Beaver Meadow, No. 5	39.08
Lackawanna	45.08
Lehigh Co's	40.05
Beaver Meadow, No. 3	40.07

COKE.

Natural of Virginia	48.08
Pittsburgh	70.09
Charcoal	104.

—FROM JOHNSON'S REPORT TO THE NAVY DEPARTMENT.

THE MECHANICAL EQUINALENT OF HEAT.

In an elaborate paper by Professor Joule, we have results thus stated :—1. The quantity of heat produced by the friction of bodies, whether solid or liquid, is always proportional to the quantity of force expended. 2. The quantity of heat capable of increasing the temperature of a pound of water by 1° Fahrenheit, requires for its evolution the expenditure of a mechanical force required by the fall of 772 pounds through the space of one foot.

Dr. Tyndall gives the following explanation of the term "foot-pounds," used as a measure by Joule:—The quantity of heat which would raise one pound of water one degree in temperature is exactly equal to what would be generated if a pound-weight after having fallen 772 feet, had its moving force destroyed by collision with the earth. Conversely, the amount of heat necessary to raise a pound of water one degree would, if applied mechanically, be competent to raise a pound-weight 772 feet high, or it would raise 772 pounds one foot high. The term "foot-pound" expresses the lifting of one pound to the height of a foot. Thus the heat required to raise the temperature of one pound of water one degree being taken as the standard, 772 foot-pounds constitute what is called *the mechanical equivalent of heat.*

ALBERT COAL.—"ALBERTITE."

Prof. Henry Wurtz, writes:—"This very remarkable material from New Brunswick is too well known to all gas engineers in the Eastern United States to require any description here. Its almost complete freedom from sulphur and from ash, and its very large yield of rich gas, makes it the most highly esteemed of all the enriching materials at present available for gas-making in the eastern portion of the United States. Unlike most cannels, its use does not sensibly impair the value of the coke produced; while it imparts, even in quantities as small as five per cent., a very satisfactory quality to the gas from common caking coals. It is not well suited to carbonization alone, owing to its highly inflammable nature, in which it resembles asphaltum. But we have obtained some results with it by the hydrocarbon process which are hereafter given."

The following results on its gas-producing powers by the common process were obtained at their experimental works by the Manhattan Gas Light Co., in New York:

Weight of charge per retort, 724lbs. Time of carbonizing, three hours and ten minutes.

Yield of gas per ton of 2,240 lbs., 14,794 feet, (equal to 6.6 feet per lb.) Illuminating power of three cubic feet burnt in a Scotch tip fish tail, 29.74 candles, equal per five cubic feet, to 49.55 candles.

Yield of coke, per ton, 14.8 bushels. Weight of coke, per ton, 806 pounds. Gas perfectly purified by lime. The coke burns well and rapidly, without clinker.

ANALYSIS OF COAL.

Volatile matter..57.70
Fixed Carbon...41.90
Ash...0.40

We deduce from this the value of one ton in lbs. of sperm equal 2811.37 lbs.

PRICES OF SCHUYLKILL COAL.

We give below the average prices for Schuylkill White Ash Coal, on board vessels at Philadelphia, from 1834 to 1872, inclusive; prepared by W. G. Neilson, and L. W. Morris, Jr.:

Years.	Prices.	Years.	Prices.
1834	$4 50	1854	$5 19
1835	4 84	1855	4 49
1836	6 84	1856	4 11
1837	6 72	1857	3 87
1838	5 27	1858	3 48
1839	5 00	1859	3 95
1840	4 01	1860	3 40
1841	5 79	1861	3 29
1842	4 18	1862	4 14
1843	3 27	1863	6 06
1844	*3 20	1864	†9 39
1845	3 46	1865	7 54
1846	3 90	1866	6 00
1847	3 80	1867	4 37
1848	3 50	1868	3 95
1849	3 62	1869	5 31
1850	3 64	1870	4 30
1851	3 34	1871	4 46
1852	3 44	1872	3 74
1853	3 70	1873	4 19

*Lowest point.   †Highest point.

COMPARATIVE YIELD OF COAL BEDS.

Comparison of yield of north and south dipping coal beds, in 1856, in Schuylkill County, Pa.

North Dip, 10 collieries, Red Ash..84,735 tons.
North Dip, 5 collieries, White Ash..91,222 tons.
South Dip, 48 collieries, Red Ash..570,561 tons.
South Dip, 26 collieries, White Ash..745,231 tons.
North and South Dip, 11 collieries, Red Ash...............................395,022 tons.
North and South Dip, 5 collieries, White Ash..............................120,101 tons.

The north dips are steeper in the Schuylkill basin than the south, and therefore more slipped and crushed, thinner and more broken. This is one of the principal arguments for the "Wave Theory of Rogers."

BREAKING STRAIN OF WIRE ROPE.

ROPES OF 133 WIRES.

	Circumference. Inches.	Diameter. Inches.	Strength. Tons.
No. 1	6¼	2¼	74.00
No. 2	6	2	65.00
No. 3	5½	1¾	54.00
No. 4	5	1½	43.60
No. 5	4½	1⅜	35.00
No. 6	4	1¼	27.20
No. 7	3½	1⅛	20.20
No. 8	3¼	1	16.00
No. 9	3	⅞	11.40
No. 10	2½	¾	8.64
No. 10½	2	⅝	5.13
No. 10⅜	1¾	9-16	4.27
No. 10¼	1½	½	3.43

—JOHN A. ROEBLING'S SONS.

WEIGHT OF T RAIL.

Weight of T rails in pounds per yard, and in tons of 2,240 pounds per mile.

At 16 pounds per yard it requires 25 tons and 325 pounds per mile.
At 18 pounds per yard it requires 28 tons and 640 pounds per mile.
At 20 pounds per yard it requires 31 tons and 660 pounds per mile.
At 22 pounds per yard it requires 34 tons and 1280 pounds per mile.
At 25 pounds per yard it requires 39 tons and 640 pounds per mile.
At 28 pounds per yard it requires 44 tons   per mile.
At 30 pounds per yard it requires 47 tons and 320 pounds per mile.
At 33 pounds per yard it requires 51 tons and 1920 pounds per mile.
At 45 pounds per yard it requires 65 tons and 960 pounds per mile.
At 48 pounds per yard it requires 75 tons and 960 pounds per mile.
At 58 pounds per yard it requires 106 tons and 1920 pounds per mile.

THE DUTY ON COAL.

There is no Anthracite imported. On Bituminous coal the duty is 75 cents per ton, gold, on the coarse coal; and on the culm of coal 40 cents per ton gold, since August 1st, 1872. Previous to that date it was $1.25 per ton, and 25 per cent. *ad valorem*, respectively.

MODES OF WORKING ADOPTED IN THE COAL MINES OF GREAT BRITAIN.

BANKS AND STRAIT WORK, BORD AND, LONGWALL.—Yorkshire.

BORD AND PILLAR.—Northumberland, North Durham, Cumberland, South Durham, North Staffordshire, Cheshire and Shropshire.

BORD AND PILLAR AND LONGWALL.—East and West Scotland.

LONGWALL.—Derbyshire, Nottinghamshire, Leicestershire, Warwickshire, South Staffordshire, *Worcestershire.

SPECIES OF BORD AND PILLAR.—North, East and West Lancashire, South Wales.

STRAIT AND STALLS.—Monmouthshire, Gloucestershire, Somersetshire, Devonshire, South Wales-
*Special method of working ten yard seam.

COAL PRODUCTION OF THE GLOBE.

COMPILED BY JAMES MACFARLANE.

The following will show the coal area of the principal coal producing countries, together with the production for the years 1870, 1871, 1872 and 1873.

	Square miles of coal.	1870.	1871.	1872.	1873.
Great Britain	11,900	110,431,192	117,352,028	123,497,816	127,016,747
United States	192,000	32,863,090	41,900,000	45,000,000	50,512,000
Germany	1,800	28,816,283	37,852,468	42,254,466	46,385,741
France	2,086	6,550,000	13,400,000	15,802,008	17,50 ,000
Belgium	900	13,697,118	13,733,176	15,666,945	17,000,000
Austria	1,800	6,443,575	9,601,350	10,333,966	11,000,000
Russia	30,000	696,209	829,722	1,097,832	1,200,000
Spain	3,501	414,482	504,060	570,060	676,000
Portugal	....	......	......	13,000	18,000
Nova Scotia	18,000	625,760	673,242	860,930	1,051,567
Australia	....	850,000	790,148	942,519	1,000,070
India	2,004	500,000	500,000	500,000	500,000
*Other countries	....	1,060,000	1,000,000	1,000,000	1,000,000
		197,398,273	236,812,194	267,775,979	273,764,085

AVERAGE CONTENTS OF COAL CARS.

The Central Railroad (of N. J.) scales at Penobscot, Luzerne Co., Pa., give the average weight of coal of each kind, and measurement of contents, as below:

    Lump..32.2 cubic feet per ton of 2240 pounds.
    Broken..35.9 cubic feet per ton of 2240 pounds.
    Egg..34.5 cubic feet per ton of 2240 pounds.
    Stove...31.8 cubic feet per ton of 2240 pounds.
    Chestnut...35.7 cubic feet per ton of 2240 pounds.
    Pea..36.1 cubic feet per ton of 2240 pounds.

FIRST USE OF COAL AS FUEL,

The Chinese, forerunners in most discoveries, knew its value centuries ago; in their own country the Romans are known to have used it, and from the twelfth century to the present day there has been an ever increasing trade in that most important of minerals. As long ago as in Edward the Sixth's reign (1552), coal was sent to France.

COAL IN SPAIN.

The area of the coal fields in Spain is set down at 2,841,505 acres; the product is about 935,000 tons of coal, and 45,000 tons lignite or brown coal, annually. The figures for 1873 being 599,707 tons of 980 lbs.—ten metric quintals. The Spanish coal fields are in the provinces of Castile, Leon and the Asturias. The process of extraction is described as being quite rude and imperfect.

VARIETIES OF COAL.

ANTHRACITE contains eighty-five to ninety-three per cent of carbon, rarely more than seven and a half per cent of volatile matter; in extreme western portion of the basin in Pennsylvania a Semi-Anthracite, containing as much as ten or fifteen per cent of volatile matter, has been found.

BITUMINOUS.—This is somewhat a deceptive term; it does not mean that any bitumen or mineral pitch, soluble in ether, is contained in it, but that the gases (oxygen, hydrogen and nitrogen) enter more largely into its composition than in Anthracite, and give it a more flaming character in burning.

SEMI-BITUMINOUS is that particular kind which, while it yields coke and combustible gases, usually contains eleven or twelve and never more than eighteen per cent of volatile combustible matter, and not less than seventy and never more than eighty-four per cent of carbon.

---

* Italy, New Zealand, Chili, China, Japan, South America and all other countries producing lignite.

UNDERGROUND HAULAGE OF COAL.

At the Hazard Collieries, near Liege, Belgium, the workings of the collieries are situated at a depth of 390 feet, and the chief bulk of the coal is drawn through an adit 3500 yards in length, the shaft being only used for men and materials and a small portion of the coal. In the adit mentioned the arrangements above named are fixed, the haulage being effected by an endless chain driven by an engine characterized by several special features.

The adit or tunnel is laid with two lines of rails, one for the out going full wagons, and another for the in going empties; these lines being 21½ in. gauge. At the outer end of the tunnel is fixed a strong girder spanning the tunnel and carrying six pulleys; the chain, as we have said, is endless, and the outgoing portion drawing the full wagons, passes over a vertical and a horizontal pulley, then off to the hauling engine. From the engine the chain returns passing round two horizontal and two vertical pulleys, crossed, and into the tunnel. At the inner end of the tunnel the chain passes around a stretching pulley, which can be adjusted by a screw. There are three curves or rather bends in the tunnel; on approaching each curve from the near end of the tunnel, the line for the loaded wagons is gradually raised with a gradient of 15 per 1000 by placing timber under the rails until the level of the latter has been raised 7¾ inches.

From this point the line is made to fall again, and at 4 ft. 11 in. from the highest place, or just at the bend of the tunnel, there is fixed a timber framing, carrying horizontal pulleys, these pulleys being so situated that the chain in passing round them is carried clear of the wagons, the latter thus pass round the bend by the action of gravity, the chain being again brought to act upon them when they arrive at the straight part of the tunnel by a depressing pulley; the chain, as will be noticed, gives motion to the wagons simply by resting on them. For the in going empties, the arrangement is exactly similar, save that the line is gradually raised as it approaches the bend from the outer end of the tunnel. The arrangement is said to have proved very efficient, and hence is well worthy of notice.

BLASTING MEMORANDA.

The following table gives the space occupied by any given quantity of powder in round holes of different sizes from one to six inches diameter:

Diameter of the hole.	Powder contained in a 1 in. hole. oz.	Powder contained in a 1 ft. hole. lb. oz.	Depth of hole to contain 1 lb powder. Inches.
One	0.1	- 5.0	38.19
One and one-half	0.9	1 11.3	17.64
Two	1.7	1 4.1	9.55
Two and one-half	2.6	1 15.4	6.11
Three	3.9	2 13.2	4.24
Three and one-half	5.1	3 13.6	3.12
Four	6.7	5 0.4	2.39
Four and one-half	8.5	6 5.8	..89
Five	10.5	7 18.7	1.53

The rules for calculating the amount of powder for a given weight is that "the charges are proportional to the cubes of the lines of least resistance," that is if from experiment we find that in a certain rock four ounces of powder is sufficient to blow out a hole where the depth of the line of least resistance from the bottom of the hole to the surface is two feet, then for one where this depth is eight feet the charge would bear the same proportion to four ounces as 2.3 does to 8.8, that is sixty-four times; it would consequently be sixteen pounds.

THE VENTILATING FURNACE.

Properly constructed furnaces, well maintained and spacious air-passages, carried well forward, will admit of an abundant flow of air along the galleries of a mine. The furnace should be placed at the bottom of the up-cast shaft, and never at the top, as is sometimes done, no matter how limited the requirements of a mine may be. Deep shaft mines never have more air than shallow ones with the same furnace power, as a deep shaft gives to a longer column of heated air. The practical power of the furnace is in proportion to the depth of the shaft, the power being as the ratio of the depth. The best place for the furnace is from 110 to 150 feet from the bottom of the up-cast shaft, as there the danger is avoided of setting the wooden structures of the shaft on fire. Many a destructive and fatal mine catastrophe has resulted from the furnace being placed in too close proximity to the wood work of the air shaft, of which the Avondale horror, was, perhaps, the most terribly destructive to human life. The passage from the furnace to the up-cast shaft should be made to slant upwards. The furnace should be of an area proportioned to the area and extent of the air passages of the mine. For an air course of 36 feet of area, a furnace of six feet in width, three feet of height above the fire bars, and from two to three feet of depth under the bars would be a fair proportion. A wide furnace is better than a high one, as it admits of a thin fire and thus more effectually heats the air in its passage through the furnace. The up-cast shaft should also be of a proper structure. Too small a shaft confines the air in passing upward, and too large a one does not get sufficiently heated by the hot ascending column of air. For an air course of 36 feet of sectional area, and a six foot furnace, the up-cast shaft should be about 30 feet. In former times it was the general practice to pass the whole of the return current of air through the furnace. In fiery mines frequent explosions occurred from the inflammable air returning to the furnace in an undiluted state. The gas would flame backwards in the mine, like a train of gunpowder, carrying death and destruction in its track. A torrent of water, called the water fall, had to be kept constantly on hand, to be thrown down the shaft to extinguish the fire. In the year 1807, Mr. Buddle had his mind intently occupied with this subject, and he devised a remedy in the dumb furnace. He split the air at the bottom of the down-cast shaft, feeding the furnace with pure air direct from the down-cast, and sending the return foul current into the up-cast shaft by a dumb drift cut in the roof above the coal. The miners were at first very much opposed to this plan, believing that the current of air by being split would lose its ventilating power. Since Mr. Buddle's time an improved dumb furnace has been made by Mr. John Smith, an intelligent mining captain, of the North of England. This furnace also fed with fresh air from the down-cast shaft, has two brick arches above the fire, for the passage of the foul return current of air into the up-cast shaft, and two air gates, one on each side of the fire to cool down the temperature between the brick work and the coal. It is only in mines subject to discharges of inflammable gas that these precautions are necessary. Unfortunately they are not as generally adopted as that necessity would seem to warrant. The Lund Hill explosion, which occurred in England, in 1853, by which 189 miners were destroyed, was believed to have been caused by the fire-damp exploding, in passing through the furnace, and an explosion from this cause occurred in a coal mine in Ohio.

THE PROPERTIES OF COMPRESSED AIR.

When air is compressed, a more rapid motion is set up among its molecules than before existed, and this increase of motion is accompanied by the development of much heat. This increase of temperature causes the air to expand, and hence introduces a force which opposes the compressing power. Thus we are enabled to account for the fact that a certain compressing force of steam or of water does not secure corresponding power in the air which is compressed. The loss of power on this account has been much diminished by improvements in the machinery used, and it is very probable that it will be much further reduced. The poor conducting power of the air makes the removal of the heat less rapid than we would wish.

If a certain volume of air is put into a smaller space, its molecules are brought closer together. This causes increased tension of the air, and thus we secure our power.

It seems that air at the highest pressure does not develop the greatest percentage of the force required to compress it. Upon this point, Wm. Daniel of Leeds, Eng., made a number of experiments. His air compressor had two steam cylinders of 16 inches diameter and 30 inches stroke, and two air cylinders of the same dimensions. The engine worked a friction brake. When the pressure of the air was 40 lbs. the useful effect on the brake was only 35½ per cent. of the power indicated on the steam gauges.

When it was 34 lbs. the useful effect was 17 per cent.
"   "   28 "   "   "   "   26 "   "
"   "   24 "   "   "   "   34 "   "
"   "   19 "   "   "   "   45½ "   "

A different relation in the dimensions of the air and steam cylinders would doubtless have affected the results.

When compared with steam, compressed air as a motive power has many advantages. It may be used at as high a pressure as steam, and in an engine neither more complicated nor more expensive. It will not condense as steam does, and for this reason is a valuable motive power when it is desired to convey it long distances.

Compressed air as a motive power has an advantage of hot air, for in doing its work it is simply regaining its natural condition.

RULES FOR USING WIRE ROPES IN DEEP SHAFTS.

The following rules will be of interest to those having occasion to use wire ropes in deep shafts:

The safe or working load should be from one-seventh to one-fifth of the breaking strain, according to the conditions under which the rope is used; the greater the vibration and velocity of the rope, the greater should be the allowance for safety.

The weight of a wire rope is about one-sixth (or .167) of a pound per cubic inch, or two pounds per foot in length per square inch section, and the proportion between the weight of a rope and its working load is as follows:

	Steel.	Charcoal Iron.
Weight per foot of rope for one ton (2000lbs.) working load	⅙ lb.	¼ lb.
Length of rope of uniform section, at which the weight of the rope is equal to its working load	6,000 ft.	4,000 ft.

Rule for finding the section at any point of a *Taper rope of uniform strength:*

S — section of rope in inches.
W — weight of wagon, cage, etc., applied at the end of the rope.
w — weight of one foot in length of the small end of the rope.
x — distance in feet from the end at which W is applied to the section S.
e — 2.7183.
f — working or safe strain in pounds per square inch section of the rope.
— 12,000 pounds for steel.
— 8,000 pounds for charcoal iron.

$$S = \frac{W}{\frac{w x}{e f} - 1}$$

The weight of the rope for x feet from the end is

$$f S - W - W \left\{ \frac{w x}{e f} - 1 \right\}$$

The working load (f) is made up of the weight applied at the end of the rope (wagon, mineral cage etc.), of the rope itself, and of the energy exerted in imparting velocity to the load. In shafts hoisting at a great speed this is an important item in the load; it is expressed by the formula,

$$\frac{W_1 V_2}{2g}, \text{ in which}$$

W_1 — the load in pounds.
V — increase in velocity in a second.
g — 32·2 — gravity.

If we take for example a shaft where $W_1 = W + W_0 = 15,000$ pounds, W_0 being the weight of the rope, the velocity attained in the first second $= V = 10$ feet, we have the energy expended in getting up this velocity,

$$\frac{W_1 V_2}{2g} = \frac{1,500,000}{64.4} = 2,329 \text{ pounds,}$$

which amount has to be added to $W + W_0$ in order to get the working strain on the rope, when we neglect the friction on the guides, the resistance of the air, rigidity of the rope, friction of sheaves on their axles, etc., which are smaller in amount, and are provided for, as is also the wear and tear of the rope, in the margin of 5 to 1 or 6 to 1, which is allowed for safety in the use of wire ropes.

TABLE FOR COMPUTING THE PRICE OF COAL.

PREPARED BY E. S. DRAKE.

LBS.	$5.50	5.75	6.00	6.25	6.50	6.75	7.00	7.25	7.50	7.75	8.00
10	3	3	3	3	3	3	4	4	4	4	4
20	6	6	6	6	7	7	7	7	8	8	8
30	8	9	9	9	10	10	11	11	11	12	12
40	11	12	12	13	13	14	14	15	15	16	16
50	14	15	15	16	16	17	18	18	19	19	20
60	17	18	18	19	20	20	21	22	23	23	24
70	19	20	21	22	23	24	25	25	26	27	28
80	22	23	24	25	26	27	28	29	30	31	32
90	25	26	27	28	29	31	32	33	34	35	36
100	29	29	30	31	33	34	35	36	39	39	40
500	1.38	1.44	1.50	1.56	1.63	1.69	1.75	1.81	1.88	1.94	2.00
1000	2.75	2.88	3.00	3.13	3.25	3.38	3.50	3.63	3.75	3.88	4.00
1500	4.13	4.32	4.50	4.69	4.88	5.07	5.25	5.44	5.63	5.82	6.00
2000	5.50	5.75	6.00	6.25	6.50	6.75	7.00	7.25	7.50	7.75	8.00

THE COAL TRADE.

COAL IN THE UNITED STATES.

The extent of the coal fields of the United States is given as 192,0'0 square miles, divided as follows:

	Square Miles.		Square Miles.
New England basin	500	Illinois basin:	
Pennsylvania Anthracite	472	Illinois section	36,800
Appalachian basin:		Indiana section	6,450
Pennsylvania section	12,8.9	West Kentucky section	3,888
Maryland section	550	Missouri basin	26,887
West Virginia section	16,000	Texas basin	4,500
Ohio section	10,000	Iowa	18,000
East Kentucky section	8,998	Nebraska	3,000
Tennessee	5,100	Kansas	17,000
Alabama	5,200	Arkansas	9,648
Michigan basin	6,700	Virginia	195
		North Carolina	810

The product keeps at about 50,000,000 tons annually, the business during the years 1873, 1874, and 1875 being, as stated below:

	1873.	1874.	1875.
Pennsylvania Anthracite	22,523,175	22,735,086	22,011,627
Pennsylvania Bituminous	11,696,858	11,088,615	11,500,080
Ohio	8,941,840	4,163,445	4,808,262
Illinois	3,500,'00	3,500,090	3,700,600
Maryland, Cumberland	2,674,100	2,410,895	2,342,773
Indiana	1,000,000	1,000,000	1,000,000
Missouri	900,000	900,060	980,000
West Virginia	600,000	600,600	600,800
Tennessee	350,000	425,000	425,000
Kentucky	300,000	400,000	425,000
Iowa	350,000	400,000	425,000
Virginia, Richmond coal field	60,000	80,000	80,0.0
Alabama	42,000	50,000	60,000
Michigan	3',000	30,00)	20,000
Kansas	50,000	75,030	75,000

WESTPHALIA.

The Westphalia coal basin of the Ruber, (Prussia) in 1873, produced 16,213,904 tons of coal, and in 1874, 15,861,131 tons.

COAL IN ITALY.

The product of coal in Italy, in 1874, was, 2,000 tons of Anthracite (?) 90,800 tons of Brown coal, and 90,000 tons of Peat coal.

EXPENSES ON BITUMINOUS COAL TO THE ATLANTIC SEA-BOARD.

West Virginia Gas Coal (Fairmount 302 miles, Clarksburg 3·1 miles) to Baltimore $4.75 per ton of 2,000 lbs. Drawback allowed on shipments to Eastern Ports, $1.20 per ton.

Pennsylvania Gas Coal from Irwin or Penn Station to West Philadelphia 332 miles. In cars of Pennsylvania Railroad Company per 2,000 lbs, $4,75.

West Virginia (Kanawha) via Chesapeake and Ohio Railroad, Blacksburg to Richmond for shipment, on Bituminous or Splint, $8.40, (special rate $8), and $1.50 (special rate $4) on Cannel.

Broad Top semi-bituminous, to Philadelphia, say 243 miles $3.20 per net ton, with a drawback of 75 cents, making toll on New York and Eastern shipments equal to $2.90 per gross ton.

George's Creek from Cumberland, Md., to Baltimore 178 miles $1.80 per 2,000 lbs. and four cents per gross ton for use of cars; from Piedmont 306 miles, $8.15 per 2,000 lbs.

George's Creek, by C. & O. Canal, from Cumberland to Georgetown, 184 miles, $1.61 per ton of 2,240 lbs., to Alexandria, Va., 191 miles, $1.69 per ton of 2,240 lbs.

From Pennsylvania State line to South Amboy, N. J., for shipment $3.00 per 2,000 lbs.

Clearfield, Pa. Bituminous, from Osceola, and other stations on the Tyrone and Clearfield branch of the Pennsylvania Railroad, to Philadelphia, say 248 miles, $4.03 per 2,000 lbs; to South Amboy 417 miles, 3.61 per 2,000 lbs. with drawback, according to destination of the coal.

George's Creek from the mines to Cumberland or Piedmont, 2 cents per ton per mile where the distance exceeds ten miles; 3 cents where the distance is from four to ten miles; and 4 cents where the distance is four miles or less.

PETROLEUM OR COAL GAS-LIGHT.

Illuminating gas as a substitute for oil and candles dates back to the early part of the present century. As a means of general illumination it has been in use in this country for about fifty years and during that entire time there seems to have been no general or abiding attempt to improve its illuminating power.

The following fundamental rules underlie the whole business:

First: *The amount of light that gas will give is dependent upon the amount of carbon it contains.*

The amount in coal gas is only from four (4) to eight (8) per cent. of its gross bulk. In oil and rosin gas it is greater.

Second: When too much gas is made from a ton of coal it contains less carbon to the foot—and consequently consumes faster than better gas.

Third: As a general statement, the larger the burner used the better the result obtained from a given quantity of gas, unless the burner is so large as to cause the gas to smoke. For example a six foot burner (a burner consuming six cubic feet of gas per hour) will give more light than two smaller burners of the same pattern consuming *four feet each* per hour, and the use of still smaller burners is still more wasteful.

Fourth: The best dry meters are not only reasonably accurate measures, when well made, but after being tested and sealed by the inspector, cannot be altered or changed in their measuring by either the company or the consumer.

Fifth: The *admixture of air or other dilutant element with gas has a still more hurtful effect* than diminishing the size of the burner. Approximately every ounce of air, when mixed in with ordinary gas destroys the lighting power of an equal weight of gas.

Sixth: Gas should not be burned at a pressure greater than one inch hydrostatic at the burner. An increase of pressure causes an increase in the amount of gas consumed, without any corresponding increase in the amount of light given.

Seventh: Ordinary coal gas (14 candles standard) compares in cost with other illuminants as follows:

The equivalents being, approximately,
1,000 feet coal gas (14 candles standard ;)
3 gallons kerosene, (as burned in a lamp ;)
49 pounds of sperm, (pure sperm candles ;)
200 feet of oil gas, (70 candles standard ;)
400 feet of rosin gas, (35 candles standard ;)
1,500 feet of "air-gas" or "gasoline gas," (10 candles standard.)

It follows that coal gas light at $3.00 per 1,000 feet, costs as much as kerosene light at $1.00 per gallon, or oil gas at $15.00 per 1,000, or sperm at six cents per pound, or rosin gas at $7.50 per 1,000, or "air gas" and "gasoline gas" at $2.00 per 1,000.

In *practically* comparing the cost of gas and coal oil a liberal allowance should be made for lamps, wicks, chimneys, &c., which will materially lessen the difference between gas light at $3.00 per 1,000 and kerosene at present prices.

COLORADO.

The area of land known to be rich in lignite coal deposits in Colorado is about 7,200 square miles, lying in various parts of the Territory, on both sides of the main range. There can hardly be a doubt but that this extent will be largely increased in years to come, for new discoveries are constantly being made upon the foot-hills and plains.

Separated under heads depending more upon their geographical position than upon the character of the fuel, we find:

1. The northern mines.
2. The eastern foot-hill mines.
3. The southern mines.
4. The Summit county mines.
5. The Conejos county mines.

Of the first but little is known. Weld and Larimer counties are undoubtedly underlain by veins of lignite similar to those of Wyoming, which are at present furnishing an excellent fuel for steam engines, domestic purposes, and for some metallurgical processes. Coke made from the product of the Wyoming coal fields has been tried at both Golden and Denver for smelting silver and gold ores, and though discarded in favor of Pennsylvania coke, is considered to be a fair fuel.

The eastern foot-hill mines embrace outcroppings in Boulder and Jefferson counties, nearly all of which have been known since the early days. They are producing at present three-fifths of all the coal mined in Colorado, which is about 120,000 tons, being located nearer the centre of population than any of the other fields.

The main workings lie mostly upon the north side of Ralston Creek, which has cut through the bed and exposed its outcroppings very markedly on either side. Nearly 2,000 feet of the vein is opened. The coal is a very good sample of the product of all the foot-hill mines. It is an altered lignite that burns freely, and crumbles quickly on exposure to the rain or moist air; burns well under the boiler and in the grate, and answers excellently for nearly all the uses to which mineral fuel is put.

The following is an analysis made in 1871, by E. W. Rollins, of the Massachusetts Institute of Technology, Boston;

```
Hydrogen.............................................  4.00 per cent.
Carbon..............................................  66.50 per cent.
Ash.................................................   7.05 per cent.
Oxygen, Nitrogen and Sulphur........................  22.45 per cent.
                                                     ---------------
                                                     100.00
```

East of Denver, along the line of the Kansas Pacific, indications of coal are not wanting. The same formation that is found along the foot-hills, tilted up in a nearly vertical position, underlies the whole of eastern Colorado, which is one vast lignite basin, containing stores of this truly precious mineral.

The southern mines embrace those of Trinidad and Fremont county, and furnish a class of mineral entirely different from any yet found in the Territory. The latter are the oldest mines and the best known, and the demand for it is great, not only for household use, but for the manufacture of gas in Denver.

The Summit county mines are not worked, as they have only lately been brought into notice. They are located on the divide between the Bear and White Rivers, and consist of several seams varying from five to fifteen feet in thickness, which owing to the contorted strata, lie in a variety of positions, from a strict horizontal to a perfect perpendicular. Above is a stratum of sandstone varying from one to three hundred feet in thickness. The coal is of two kinds, one a hard lignite and the other similar to what is called albertite.

The Conejos beds are also now discoveries of which but little is known. Sufficient outcroppings of coal, however, have been noticed below, and west of Las Animas or Elbert, to indicate the existence of extensive lignite deposits there. The mines are hardly opened yet, but situated as they are, not more than thirty miles south of the centre of the San Juan gold and silver district, it will be but a short time before their product will be called for, should they prove at all suitable for metallurgical purposes.—*Colorado Mining Review.*

THE COAL TRADE.

COAL IN INDIANA.

The area of the Indiana coal measures approximates one-fifth of the entire State, and embraces the Counties of Perry, Spencer, Warwick, Posey, Vanderburg, Gibson, Pike, Dubois, Daviess, Knox, Martin, Sullivan, Greene, Clay, Vigo, Parke, Vermilion and Fountain. The most important coals, from a manufacturing point of view, are those known as the "lower block" 3.8 thick, the "main block" 4.4 thick, and "upper block" 1.10 thick. Block coal has a laminated structure, and is composed of alternate thin layers of vitreous dull black coal and fibrous mineral charcoal. It splits readily into sheets, breaking with difficulty in the opposite direction; on burning, it scarcely swells, or changes form, and never cakes or runs together. What the celebrated English chemist, Mushet, said about a certain Welsh coal, is equally applicable to the block coal of Indiana. To the purity of splint coal it unites all the softness and combustability of wood, and the effects produced by it in the blast furnace, either as to the quality or quantity of iron, far exceed everything in the manufacture of that metal with charcoal. From careful assays, it is ascertained that this coal gives from 56 to 62 per cent. of fixed carbon, a small amount of water and a small amount of ash. Dr. E. T. Cox, the State geologist, gives this coal an exceptional character as an iron smelting fuel, and reports a ton of pig iron as being made with 4,250 pounds of block coal.

The coal in Clay County is favorably known as an iron-smelting fuel, and we append a description of its qualities. "There are two veins of coal, the upper vein averaging about three feet ten inches in thickness, and the lower one averaging about four feet. The roof is principally sand rock, slate, and slate and sand rock mixed. Fire and potters' clay of good quality underlie the coal. The average depth to the first vein is about forty-five feet from the surface, and the second or lower vein is found at an average depth of seventy-five to eighty feet. The coal is free from slate and sulphur. It burns freely, and leaves a soft, fine white ash, similar to wood ash, and no clinkers." For domestic and steam purposes, this coal is largely used in Chicago, Ill; Indianapolis, Ind; Kalamazoo, Mich.; and the towns and stations along the lines of most of the railroads leading from this coal district, among which may be mentioned the St. Louis, Vandalia, Terre Haute and Indianapolis Railroad; the Jeffersonville, Madison and Indianapolis Railroad; the Indianapolis and St. Louis Railroad; the Louisville, New Albany and Chicago Railroad; the Cincinnati, Lafayette and Chicago Railroad; the Lake Shore and Michigan Southern Railroad; the Indianapolis, Decatur and Springfield Railroad; and the Michigan Central Railroad.

In the block coal zone of the Indiana coal fields there are as many as eight seams of non-caking coal, four of which are of good workable thickness over a portion of the field. These are I, G, F and A, which together, have a maximum thickness of fifteen feet; and by including the other four seams, we have six feet more, making a total of twenty-one feet of block coal.

The coal of Parke County is favorably reported on for the manufacture of iron. It is a block coal, averaging five feet in thickness, weighing seventy-seven pounds to the cubic foot, and gives by analysis 62.5 fixed carbon, 31.00 volatile matter, 4.05 water, and 2 per cent. of ash. The estimated area is about 800 square miles of workable coal.

The "upper block" at Washington, in Daviess County, is extensively mined; and meets with a ready market at St. Louis, and all the towns on the Ohio and Mississippi Railroad. Its specific gravity is 1.294; a cubic foot weighs 80.87 pounds; by analysis it yields: fixed carbon, 60.00; ash, 4.50; volatile matter, 35.50. The coal worked is known as L, a five foot seam of Bituminous, an excellent caking coal, free from impurities, and may be handled and stocked without much loss; it has been used for gas making at St. Louis, and is a three foot ten inch seam of very pure coal, jet black, of cubical fracture, and bears a good reputation as a fuel, for general uses.

The census report for 1870 shows the product of coal for the year 1869 to have been 437,870 tons. The output for the year 1875 is estimated at 1,500.000 for the whole State.

MECHANICAL STOKER.

Firing apparatus, fuel-feeders, or mechanical stokers have been experimented upon for some time. A new one, recently tried with success upon a battery of marine boilers, presents some features of interest. It consists of a flat hopper placed above the fire door and before the boiler, and a mechanical device for grinding and injecting the coal. The hopper may be of any desired size. For stationary boilers, it might hold a ton or more; for marine boilers, this would depend upon the available room. The hopper ends below in an adjustable box, that may be enlarged; or diminished in size as the nature of the fuel demands. In this box is a feed and crushing roller that breaks up the coal into dust or slack, and drops it below into a flat iron box holding two horizontal discs turning in opposite directions. The stream of slack or dust coal falling between these opening discs is shot forward through an opening into the fire-box.

By the use of this stoker, a fine shower of broken coal is continually spread over the entire surface of the grate-bars, and by governing the speed of the apparatus, the supply of fuel is regulated to suit the demand for steam. To prevent the fuel from caking into a mass of clinkers on the fire, every alternate grate-bar is given an up-and-down and two-and-fro motion, that gradually breaks up the clinkers, and forces them forward upon a balanced plate that may be upset by the fireman, and the waste dropped into the ash pit. The top of each bar is notched so as to cause the clinkers to catch and travel in one direction. All parts of the apparatus are outside of the fire-box, and there is no injury from heating and burning.

The valuable points claimed for this machine are freedom from cold currents over the fire, as there are no doors to be opened; freedom from smoke as the combustion is more perfect; and the use of small, inferior and slack coal—with the same steam results. Another result claimed is the increased comfort of the fire-room in point of temperature, as the fire door is kept constantly closed. On one steamship where this stoker was tried, the saving in cost of fuel was marked. The first voyage with hand-stoking lasted 53 days 13 hours under steam, with a consumption of 684 tons of coal, valued at £573 19s. The second voyage lasted 52 days 11 hours, and the consumption of fuel by the use of the mechanical stoker was 619 tons of slack and 87 tons of coal, at a total expense of £578 0d.

MINE DRAINAGE.

The matter of mine drainage resolves itself into a three fold question of cost, convenience, and durability of the working conditions, whether permanent or temporary. It is believed that the drainage of mines would inevitably develop upon the simple, powerful and effective "Special" class. An illustration of a few examples of deep single lift engines, which had been placed in mines in most cases in pairs. A pair at Suffield Colliery, 24-inch steam cylinder, 7-inch pump cylinder, and 48 strokes per minute, raised each 10,000 gallons per hour in a single lift of 825 feet. A pair at Wigan, 30-inch steam cylinder, with 10-inch pump, at 48 strokes, raised each 20,000 gallons per hour 500 feet. Two at Newcastle, 32-inch cylinder, 7-inch pump, 72 strokes per minute, each raised 10,-000 gallons per hour in a single lift of 1,048 feet. These were approximate statements of duty at 100 feet of piston speed per minute. At least 2,000 of these pumps are now at work in various British and foreign mines. The system of direct acting pumping engines was even more important, however, as affecting the drainage of new mining undertakings. For this purpose the "Special" pump was peculiarly fitted by its compact and complete character. One very important feature was that the direct acting steam pump of this type could be put down in pairs, while Cornish engines could not. Hence, whenever a mishap occurred, causing the stoppage of the engine, the whole of the pumping ceased, which, of course, was not the case when the engines were in duplicate.

PETROLEUM AS FUEL.

Sainte-Claire Deville, experimenting for the French Government, found in oil from Oil Creek which will pretty fairly represent average American crude petroleum, a total calorific power of 9,963 centigrade units, equal to the evaporation of 16.16 lbs. of steam per pound of oil, and he was able practically to evaporate 14.05 lbs. with a pound of this petroleum. Now, a pound of pure, dry charcoal has a total theoretical heat of 7,990 units, and the oil thus has a greater evaporative power by just about 25 per cent. A gallon of petroleum weighs about 6½ pounds, so a gallon has the heating power of 8½ pounds of pure charcoal, and barrel of 49 gallons is equivalent to 390 lbs. of such charcoal, and 6½ barrels of oil are equivalent to one long ton of charcoal.

Pure, dry charcoal, however, is hardly to be got except for chemical experiments, and the ordinary charcoal of commerce has only about three-fourths as great heating power. Not being used to make steam, it need not be considered further.

The theoretical heating power of the best British coals is given as between 14 and 15 lbs. of steam per pound of coal, or nearly as great as that of petroleum; but the great advantage claimed for petroleum is the nearly complete utilization of its heating power, owing to its perfect and even composition, and the easy management of the heat arising from it. Thus the best practical results of the British Admiralty experiments with the best coal was the evaporation of 9.5 lbs. of steam per lb. of best coal, while Sainte-Claire Deville evaporated 14.05 lbs. with a pound of petroleum, and Professor Wurtz says, "with perfect combustion and skilled handling, we may safely adopt, as the actual steam value of our petroleum, fifteen pounds of water made into steam by one pound of oil." This is just 100 lbs. per gallon of oil.

By United States Navy experiments, Lackawanna Anthracite evaporated 9.8 lbs of water per lb. of coal; Cumberland Bituminous 9.44 lbs.; and Pittsburgh Bituminous (which is most likely to come into competition with petroleum) 8.2 lbs. On this basis:

$$1 \text{ gallon oil} = 10.2 \text{ lbs. Lackawanna.}$$
$$= 10.6 \text{ lbs. Cumberland.}$$
$$= 12.2 \text{ lbs. Pittsburgh.}$$

and a long ton of

Lackawanna = 219.6 gallons petroleum.
Cumberland = 211.3 " "
Pittsburgh = 183.6 " "

This, be it remembered, is the comparison of the actual effectiveness of the coals used in the navy experiments with the almost perfect utilization of the heating power which Professor Wurtz anticipates from the use of petroleum. Given the prices of coal and assuming the correctness of the statements made by the advocates of petroleum, it will be easy to ascertain which is the most economical fuel, where steam is made under advantageous circumstances. With the best coal above named, about five barrels of petroleum will take the place of a ton of coal, with the poorest, about 4¼ barrels.

The claims of the advocates of petroleum, however, are not only placed on the practicability of the more complete utilization of the total heating power of the liquid fuel, but of its practicability under circumstances where coal is very imperfectly utilized. For instance, they claim that such complete, or nearly complete utilization is practicable in locomotives, where coal, we know, is not so effective as in furnaces with larger heating surface where the fire is less violently urged. One of the peculiarities claimed for petroleum is its availability for making an intense heat without waste, either by non-combustion of particles or the escape of a great part of the heat up the chimney. Further, the perfect combustion of petroleum, leaving neither coal nor cinders, is advanced as a recommendation of the fuel where these products of ordinary coal fires become a nuisance, as in most engines in cities and especially in locomotives designed for use in city streets.

All these comparisons, it must not be forgotten, are made on the assumption that a pound of crude petroleum will evaporate 15 pounds of water—will do the best work claimed for it by those who advocate its use; and the chief value of the figures [given will be to show where petroleum cannot, rather than where it can be economical.

COAL IN WESTERN KENTUCKY.

The coal field west of the Louisville and Nashville Railroad was first developed during the year 1872. The markets for the coal are Nashville, Tenn., and points on line of railroad from Evansville, Ind., to Nashville, Tenn. There are twelve veins of coal, ranging from two feet to eight feet in thickness. For steam purposes the coal rates at 99, Pittsburgh coal being a hundred. For gas purposes four feet to the pound is obtained, but there is more sulphur than in Pittsburgh coal.

TEMPERING MINING PICKS.

There is probably no service to which steel can be put, which so effectually tests its value, as in mining picks. The tempering of a pick is a very nice piece of work and should be done with great care. In the first place a good charcoal fire is necessary; next, good steel, add then a good light hammer with a smooth-face anvil; and lastly a man is needed with a good keen eye, considerable experience and excellent judgement. No good pick can be turned out if any of the above essentials are wanting in the process. A pick should never be „upset," or hammered endwise, nor raised above a full red heat. The steel should be, moreover, heated as quickly as possible, as long exposure to heat—even if the heat is not in excess—injures its texture. Many blacksmiths find great difficulty in tempering picks, because they do not choose good steel. After being heated the pick must be worked with care, special pains being taken in drawing it out, to hammer on all sides alike, in one place as much as another, and one side as much as the other. When ready for hardening, it should be heated in the blaze of a charcoal fire until red hot, and then plunged into cold rain water, and kept there until it is nearly cold; but if kept too long in the water or until it is quite cold the corners are liable to fall off. Some blacksmiths use hot water: no salts of any kind should exist in the water but the water should be cold; if the water is warm and a little ice should be thrown in to chill it, the tempering will be all the better. Pure soft water for hardening will make a tougher pick, and one less liable to crack at the edges than where salt water is used. An old mining partner of the writers, who always sharpened the picks at the claim, and was quite experat it, used to hold the pick end in the water for just exactly a certain length of time until a certain shade of color appeared. Then he did not consider it properly tempered until the point was inverted in the ground and allowed to gradually cool. The last hammering of a pick should always be given on the flat sides, across close to the edges and then up each side about an inch. By so doing the corners will be less liable to crack off.

COAL IN NORTHUMBERLAND COUNTY, PA.

The following is the quantity of coal mined and sent to market from Northumberland county; in 1875, by the different operators in that region:

Collieries.	Operators.	Tons.
Cameron	Mineral R. R. & M. Co.	27,790
Big Mountain	Patterson, L. & Co.	19,183
Buck Ridge	May, Audenried & Co.	110,287
Burnside	Isaac May & Co.	108,521
Luke Fidler	Mineral R. R. & Mining Co.	103,891
Bear Valley	A. A Heim & Goodwill	91,977
Henry Clay	J. Langdon & Co.	85,941
Trevorton	P. & R. C. & I. Co.	76,390
Hickory Swamp	Mineral R. R. & Mining Co.	70,594
Enterprise	Enterprise Coal Co.	52,765
Monitor	G. W. Johns.	48,348
B. Franklin	Douty & Baumgarnder.	46,908
Stuartville	Wm. Momtelius.	44,604
Excelsior	Excelsior Mining Co.	43,468
Reliance	Reliance Coal Co.	34,931
Geo. Fales	A. A. Heim & Goodwill.	32,577
Locust Spring	P. & R. C. I. Co.	31,736
Lancaster	Smith & Keiser.	24,864
Alaska Shaft	P. & R. C. & I. Co.	21,398
Morton	Thomas Morton.	20,604
Greenback	Guiterman, Gorman & Co.	20,577
Hickory Ridge	Mineral R. R. & Mining Co.	18,040
Locust Gap	Graeber & Kemple.	18,891
Helfenstein	P. & R. C. & I. Co.	15,973
Coal Ridge	Burton Bros. & Co.	12,412
Franklin	Lover, Booth & Elms.	10,669
Black Diamond	Schwenk & Co.	4,266
Marshall	Reese and Brother.	2,919
Royal Oak	Tillet & Brother.	800
Lambert	William Brown.	170
Total for 1875		1,628,683
Total for 1874		1,221,551
Increase in 1875		417,132

THE WORKING COST OF COLLIERIES.

We publish the following estimate, showing a comparison of the working cost of certain English collieries in 1870 and 1874. It is said to have been made after a very careful examination of all available information:—

WORKING COST FOR 1870

	£	s.	d.
Wages for one year for 209 collieries	1,064,999	14	2
Keep of 3040 horses, at 10s. 6d. per week for one year	82,542	0	0
Keep of 6996 ponies, at 6s. 6d. per week for one year	197,923	8	0
Hewers—22,500,000 tons, at 1s. per ton	1,175,000	0	0
Royalty— do " 6d. "	587,500	0	0
Props and plates—22,500,000 tons at 1d. per ton	97,916	13	4
Wear and tear—22,500,000 tons at 1d. per ton	97,916	13	4
Total expenses for 1870	3,514,248	8	11
Increase of expenses of 1874 over 1870	1,414,261	2	2
Add for sundry expenses that may be omitted	500,00	0	0
	£5,414,261	2	2

WORKING COST FOR 1874.

	£.	s.	d.
Wages for one year for 209 collieries	2,250,949	11	9
Keep of 8040 horses, at 13s. per week for one year	102,752	0	0
Keep of 6386 ponies, at 8s. per week for one year	132,828	16	0
Hewers—23,500,000 tons, at 1s. 6¼d. per ton	1,786,979	3	4
Royalty—23,500,000 tons, at 9d. per ton	881,250	0	0
Props and plates—23,500,000 tons at 1½d. per ton	146,875	0	0
Wear and tear—23,500,000 tons at 1½d. per ton	146,875	0	0
Workmen's coals—500,000 tons at 6s. per ton	150,000	0	0
Total expenses for 1874	5,723,509	11	0

THE
COAL TRADE JOURNAL,

PUBLISHED EVERY WEDNESDAY.

The only Newspaper in the United States entirely devoted to the Coal Interests.

ESTABLISHED - - APRIL 21, 1869.

SUBSCRIPTION, $2.50 A YEAR, POSTAGE INCLUDED; PAYABLE STRICTLY IN ADVANCE.

Communications bearing upon the coal industry solicited.

Advertising rates made known on application.

Checks or Post Office Orders are preferable methods of payment, and should be to the order of the proprietor.

FREDERICK E. SAWARD,

EDITOR AND PROPRIETOR.

Publication Office, No. 111 Broadway.

THE COAL TRADE JOURNAL

is the acknowledged authority on the subject of coal. RELIABLE, PROMPT, CORRECT, INDEPENDENT. No clique, or class of dealers control its columns. It is not local; facts and figures from all parts of America and Europe. The business done in coal at every principal city, prices, tonnage, qualities dealt in, fully shown. New routes to the coal fields and new processes in the economy of fuel form an important feature of this journal.

ITS CIRCULATION IS UNIVERSAL.

going as it does, weekly, to every dealer in coal throughout the

UNITED STATES, THE BRITISH PROVINCES IN NORTH AMERICA, AND TO GREAT BRITAIN.

Back numbers and bound volumes can be supplied.

———:o:———

If more convenient subscribers may hand their favors to the following gentlemen, who will be pleased to receive and forward them.

JOSEPH O. GINN, 23 Doane St., Boston.   A. W. MCALPINE, Wilkesbarre, Pa.
SHAW BROS., 24 2nd St., Baltimore, Md.   FRANK W. BALCH, 280 Madison St., Chicago, Ill.
W. H. SMITH & SONS, 186 Strand, London, Eng.

W. H. MEEKER, New York.   JOSEPH F. DEAN, Boston.

—o—

MEEKER & DEAN,

MINERS AND SHIPPERS,

OF

Lackawanna & Wyoming Valley,

COAL,

111 BROADWAY, NEW YORK, & 23 DOANE STREET, BOSTON.

We invite the attention of dealers and consumers to the following varieties of coal, **OF WHICH WE HAVE THE EXCLUSIVE SALE,** in this market, and solicit correspondence,

Lackawanna Valley,   FREE BURNING WHITE ASH.
Kingston,   WYOMING WHITE ASH.
Chauncey,   WYOMING RED ASH.

ALSO,

Cross Creek,   LEHIGH RED ASH.
Beaver Brook,   LEHIGH WHITE ASH.

—o—

Shipments made at Hoboken, N. J., always accessible and advantageous in point of freight charges.

—o—

Vessels and Boats Chartered at the Lowest Rates, and Prompt Despatch Given in Loading.

GEORGE'S CREEK CUMBERLAND COAL.

THE NEW CENTRAL COAL COMPANY'S MINES.

Experiments were made by the Superintendent of the United States Armory at Springfield Mass., during 1873, to test the value of certain coals as steam generators with the following results:

	Lackawanna.	Pittston.	Cumberland.
Pound per h. p. per hour	4.01	4.02	3.03
Cost per Gross ton	$8.05	$7.85	$9.10
Cost per horse power	1 5-10 cts.	1 4-10 cts.	1 2-10 cts.

Each variety was used for six consecutive days; and it is therefore alleged that bituminous coal from the Cumberland region is the most economical fuel as a steam generator, making more heat and creating more power per pound, and per cent, of cost than the harder coal.

The reputation of the 14 feet George's Creek vein of Cumberland coal is now fully established, and it is conceded to be unequalled for steam generating purposes. It is supplied to every European and coastwise steamer which leaves this port; to almost every railroad, not only in New York, but through the Eastern, Middle, and some of the Southern States. It is burned upon most of the ferry boats, and a great number of the factories, foundries, glass works, etc., in New England and New York. Its superiority for all these various purposes of manufacture and commerce is so generally conceded that the demand is steadily increasing.

The lands and mines of the *New Central Coal Company* are located in the heart of the region, and comprise between three and four thousand acres, on which openings have already been made, developing 1,100 acres of the fourteen foot bed, the coal from which has proved itself the very best in the Cumberland region. The facilities of the Company are among the best, and their rank as producers is shown in the fact that for three years past they have sold and delivered an average of 325,000 tons each year.

The Company solicit orders from consumers in coal for steam raising, and will continue to furnish first-class coal, shipped either from Baltimore, Md.; Georgetown, D. C.; Hoboken, N. J.; or South Amboy, N. J.

Prompt deliveries may be relied upon.

The Offices of the *New Central Coal Company* are at Rooms 6 and 6½ Trinity Building, 111 Broadway, New York.

HARRY CONRAD, President.   S. F. BARGER, Vice President.
P. O. CALHOUN, Treasurer.   WM. S. JACQUES, Secretary.
MALCOLM SINCLAIR, General Manager.

SALES AGENTS:

B. O. Thwing & Co.,	L. S. Boyer & Co.,	ISAAC T. HOTCHKISS,
77 State Street,	236 Dock Street,	111 Broadway,
Boston, Mass.	Phila.	New York.

H. H. SHILLINGFORD, Pres't.   H. T. SHILLINGFORD, Sec. and Treas.

KITTANING COAL COMPANY,

MINERS AND SHIPPERS OF

BITUMINOUS COAL.

For Steam, Rolling Mills, Blacksmithing, Glass Works, Brick and Lime Burning, Coking.

GENERAL OFFICE,
125 SOUTH FOURTH STREET,
PHILADELPHIA,

SHIPPING PIERS.

Greenwich Point, Phila.; South Amboy, N. J.; Canton, Baltimore.

THE KITTANING COAL COMPANY

Own about *eight thousand acres* and control by lease about *one thousand acres* of Bituminous Coal territory in what is known by geologists as the Moshannon Coal Basin, in the counties of Clearfield and Centre, State of Pennsylvania, and which is designated in the recent report of the second Geological Survey of the State, as the *Steam Coal Basin of Clearfield County*. The territory lies on both sides of the Moshannon stream, which is the dividing line between the two counties named, and the dip of the coal on both sides of the Valley being towards said stream. There are known to exist on the property five explored beds of coal, laid down by geologists as A, B, C, D and E. The bed B, as mentioned in the State Geological Survey report, but by other geologists laid down as D, is the only one at present developed and worked by the Company; it is about five and a half feet in thickness, of pure, clean coal. The Geological Survey Department of the State gives the following analysis of the coal. Water at 225° F., 670; Volatile matter, 21.360; Fixed Carbon, 74.284; Sulphur, .435; Ash, 3.151. Coke per cent., 77.97. Color of Ash, cream.

The following remarks are appended to the analysis:
"The coal is undoubtedly a most excellent one, and admirably adapted for STEAM PURPOSES as well as for use in IRON MANUFACTORIES."

Charles A. Seely, Chemist, of New York, gives the following analysis of the same coal:
One hundred parts contain

Volatile combustible matter.. 20.10
Fixed Carbon... 76.39
Ash... 3.51

100.000

Coke, 89.09. The sample contained of sulphur, 0.19.

The reports of the consumers of this coal of its practical working result, show more favorably its superiority than the foregoing analysis indicate.

Outside of the property of this Company comparatively but little of this bed of coal is known to exist, or at least none known to be accessible to market by the present facilities.

DIRECTORS.

CHAS. W. TROTTER,   GEORGE HOWELL,
H. N. BURROUGHS,   CHAS. W. POULTNEY,
ZOPHAR C. HOWELL.   A. J. DERBYSHIRE,
H. H. SHILLINGFORD.

MINE LOCOMOTIVES.

Among others, the following parties are now operating Mine Locomotives built by PORTER, BELL & Co., of Pittsburgh, Pa.:

IN THE BITUMINOUS COAL REGION OF PENNSYLVANIA.

The Westmoreland Coal Co.; 1¾ miles underground road; heaviest, grade 200 feet per mile. Saxman & Co., Latrobe, 185 feet grade Jones & Laughlins, Pittsburgh, 141 feet grade. H. B. Hays & Bro., Pittsburgh.

IN THE ANTHRACITE REGIONS.

Lehigh Coal and Navigation Co., Susquehanna Coal Co.

IN THE CUMBERLAND REGION, MARYLAND.

Consolidation Coal Co.; 2½ and 3 miles underground roads, grades 115 and 185 feet. George's Creek Coal and Iron Co., 212 and 265 feet grades.

IN THE HOCKING VALLEY REGION, OHIO.

Hayden & Son; W. B. Brooks; New York and Ohio Coal Co.

IN IOWA.

Union Coal and Mining Co.; Fort Dodge Coal Co.

The running expenses of a Mine Locomotive, including wages, fuel, repairs and interest, are about the same as of three mules and three drivers, and the work done from three to ten times greater; keeping up footpath while works are running, and feeding mules when works are shut down, are other disadvantages of animal power.

PORTER, BELL & Co make Light Locomotives, their exclusive specialty, and have a great variety of sizes and styles, from five to twenty tons weight and twenty eight to sixty inches gauge of track, at work at coal, iron, lumber and other operations, and on narrow gauge railroads throughout the United States, and in Canada, Cuba, and South America.

TO COAL CONSUMERS:

NEW YORK, April, 1876.

During the season of 1876, I shall be pleased to receive your orders for any of the following popular coals:

OLD COMPANY'S LEHIGH, FROM SUMMIT HILL MINES,

HONEY BROOK SUPERIOR WHITE ASH LEHIGH,

PLYMOUTH WYOMING—RED ASH,

WILKESBARRE COAL (BALTIMORE VEIN),

FULTON LEHIGH,

DELAWARE, LACKAWANNA & WESTERN CO.'S SCRANTON,

PHILADELPHIA & READING COAL & IRON COMPANY'S SCHUYLKILL COALS,

GEORGE'S CREEK CUMBERLAND COAL, FROM THE WELL KNOWN HAMPSHIRE MINES.

My friends throughout New York and New England may rely upon receiving the same uniform quality of coal, and promptness in filling their orders, as during past seasons.

Shipments made to all points accessible from New York, and at favorable rates of freight.

Address,

FRED. A. POTTS,

110 BROADWAY, NEW YORK,

33 WESTMINSTER STREET, PROVIDENCE, R. I.

Geo. W. Huntzinger, President.   John B. Garrett, Treasurer.
T. C. Trotter, Secretary.

PHILADELPHIA COAL CO.,

MINERS AND SHIPPERS OF

LEHIGH AND LOCUST MOUNTAIN,

230 SOUTH SECOND STREET, PHILADELPHIA.

WM. BORDEN.   L. N. LOVELL.

BORDEN & LOVELL,

Cumberland Coal,

From the Borden Mines and the Borden Shaft.

FOR RAILROAD, STEAMSHIP AND GENERAL USES.

UNEXCELLED IN QUALITY BY ANY FROM THIS REGION.

SHIPMENTS MADE AT

Georgetown, D. C., Baltimore, Md., South Amboy, N. J.

Offices—Nos. 70 and 71 West Street, New York.

AGENTS FOR THE SALE OF

FALL RIVER IRON WORKS COMPANY'S NAILS, BANDS, HOOPS AND RODS.

Lehigh & Wilkesbarre Coal Co.

OLD CO'S SUMMIT LEHIGH,
WILKESBARRE, From the Baltimore Vein.
PLYMOUTH RED ASH,
HONEY BROOK LEHIGH.

Orders solicited. Coal shipped at Port Johnston, N. J., promptly and in good order.

OFFICE, 80 BROADWAY, NEW YORK.
JOHN F. WILSON, General Sales Agent.

PHILADELPHIA AND READING

COAL AND IRON COMPANY,

GENERAL OFFICE:

227 SOUTH FOURTH STREET, PHILADELPHIA,

OFFER

HARD AND FREE BURNING WHITE ASH COALS,

SCHUYLKILL RED ASH,

SHAMOKIN, NORTH FRANKLIN, LORBERRY, AND LYKENS VALLEY COAL,

ON BOARD AT

Port Richmond, Philadelphia, or foot of North 9th St., Brooklyn, for Delivery in New York, and all Ports Along the Sound and Hudson River.

Circulars of Prices will be issued monthly.

NEW YORK OFFICE—9 BROAD STREET, DREXEL BUILDING.

E. A. QUINTARD, General Sales Agent.

Keystone Coal and Manuf'g Co.,

OFFICE;

No. 10 Merchants Exchange, Philadelphia,

MINERS AND SHIPPERS OF

CUMBERLAND COAL.

H. A. STILES, President.

—o—

ORDERS PROMPTLY FILLED.

—o—

L. S. BOYER & CO., 228 Dock Street, Philadelphia, Agents for *NEW ENGLAND STATES.*

E. GULAGER.   GEO. TUTHILL.   C. GULAGER.

EDWARD GULAGER & CO.,

Successors to

SAMUEL BONNELL, JR.,

Honey Brook Lehigh Coal, also, *Red and White Ash Wyoming.*

DELIVERED ON BOARD OF VESSELS AT PERTH AMBOY AND PORT JOHNSTON, N. J.

OFFICES:

43 and 45 Trinity Building, 111 Broadway, New York.

Shipping Piers, - - - - - - { Greenwich, Philadelphia.
{ South Amboy, New Jersey.

R. B. WIGTON,

Miner and Shipper of best Quality of

BITUMINOUS COAL

For Rolling Mills, Locomotives, Steamers, Glass Works, Brick and Lime Burning,
Smithing and Steam Generating Purposes.

"MORRISDALE" and "CUNARD."

OFFICE, 203 SOUTH FOURTH STREET, PHILADELPHIA,

BRANCH OFFICE, Rooms 51 and 52, 71 Broadway, N. Y.

JOSEPH W. JOHNSTON, Agent.

The following are a few of the very satisfactory reports that have been received from consumers:

PENNSYLVANIA STEEL WORKS. "Superior to much of the coal from the district and inferior to none."

N. J. STEEL & IRON CO. "None so uniformly satisfactory."

PHŒNIX IRON CO. "A first class coal in every respect."

PAXTON ROLLING MILL. "Giving better results than Cumberland, no clinker and free burning."

HUSTON & PENROSE. "After trying best veins of Cumberland, we give it the preference."

WM. L. BAILEY & CO. "Used it with uniform satisfaction for many years."

NORRISTOWN IRON WORKS. "Gives entire satisfaction, used for years."

FULTON ROLLING MILL. "Better suited for puddling and more economical than any other."

STONEY CREEK IRON WORKS. "We think the Morrisdale superior to any other vein in Pennsylvania."

GRAYS' FERRY IRON WORKS. "After using Cumberland for many years, was induced to try Morrisdale, which I prefer to use."

Further reference is made to the Architectural Iron Works, Quintard Iron Works, the Morgan Iron Works, New York City, who use this coal exclusively. Also to the Charleston S. S. Co., and Morgan and West India lines of steamers and others which want of space prohibits quoting.

NEW YORK AND CLEVELAND

GAS COAL COMPANY,

OF PITTSBURGH, PA.

MINERS AND SHIPPERS OF

YOUGHIOGHENY GAS COAL.

This company is prepared to furnish any quantity of their justly celebrated and acknowledged superior GAS COAL, to any point reached by railroad or navigation, on most favorable terms.

GENERAL OFFICE, 89 WOOD STREET, PITTSBURGH, PA.

BRANCH OFFICE, 130 WATER STREET, CLEVELAND, OHIO.

WILLIAM A. MCINTOSH, Pres't.   A. CARNEGIE, Vice-Pres't.   W. P. DEARMIT, Treas.

THOMAS AXWORTHY, AGENT, - - CLEVELAND, OHIO.

W. H. WATERBURY, SALES AGENT,   137 BROADWAY, NEW YORK.

James H. Dysart, Altoona.   Daniel Laughman, Altoona.   W. H. Piper, Philadelphia.

DYSART & COMPANY,

SOLE PROPRIETORS, MINERS AND SHIPPERS OF

SONMAN BITUMINOUS COAL.

SHIPPING WHARVES,

CANTON, BALTIMORE, MD.,
GREENWICH POINT, PHILA.,
SOUTH AMBOY, NEW JERSEY.

General Office, 314½ WALNUT STREET, PHILADELPHIA.

---o---

This coal is of superior quality for General Steam Uses, Blacksmithing, etc., the SMALL coal being separated and used for a special purpose, none but the LUMP COAL is sent eastward for shipment, thus making this coal, an especially recommendable coal, for use and shipment.

ALL ORDERS PROMPTLY FILLED, AND SATISFACTION GUARANTEED.

PENN GAS COAL COMPANY,

OFFER THEIR COAL,

Carefully Prepared and Screened for Gas Purposes.

Their property is located in the Youghiogheny Coal Basin, near Irwin's and Penn Stations, on the Pennsylvania Railroad, and on the Youghiogheny River,

WESTMORELAND COUNTY, PA.

---o---

PLACES OF SHIPMENT:

Pennsylvania Railroad Pie. No. 2 (lower side), Greenwich Wharves, Delaware River. Pier No. 1 (lower side), South Amboy, N. J.

---o---

OFFICES:

No. 90 WALL STREET, NEW YORK.
No. 11 Merchants Exchange, Philadelphia.

CANNELTON COAL CO.,
OF WEST VIRGINIA,

Offer for sale the following Coals, from their colliery at CANNELTON, Kanawha County, West Virginia, shipped at Richmond, Va.

CANNELTON CANNEL,

acknowledged to be the BEST ENRICHER produced in this country, a gross ton yielding 10,000 cubic feet of Gas, 64.54 candle power. COKE, 32 Bushels—Good Quality.

CANNELTON CAKING COAL.

a superior coal for Gas Manufacture, a gross ton yielding 10,700 cubic feet of Gas, of 16^{14-100} candle power. Coke, 41 bushels, weighing 1,456 lbs., good quality. Sulphur, 1½ per cent. and Ash 2 per cent.

CANNELTON SEMI-CANNEL.

producing 11,220 cubic feet of Gas—22 candle power—1,300 lbs. of Coke.

SPLINT AND BLOCK COALS.

These are superior House or Steam Coals—making little or no slack in transportation—excellent substitutes for Cannel for use in open grates.

J. TATNALL LEA, Treasurer,
P. O. BOX 1747. PHILADELPHIA

SALE AGENTS { PERKINS & JOB, 27 South St., N. Y. and 91 State St., Boston. H. W. BENEDICT & SON, New Haven.

Franklin Coal of Lykens Valley and Cameron Coal of Shamokin.

The agents appointed to sell the product of all collieries managed by the undersigned are as follows:

For New England, New York, New Jersey and south of Cape Henry, the City of Philadelphia, and the line trade of the Philadelphia and Reading Railroad.

GENERAL AGENTS—SINNICKSON & CO., 201 WALNUT STREET, PHILADELPHIA, Sub Agents. ELISHA MOSELY, 82 Water Street, Boston. WM. M. ROGERS, 65 Trinity Building, New York. B. W. PERSONS, 39 Weybosset Street, Providence, Rhode Island.

For all other points than those above named; General Agents. HALL BROTHERS & CO., 3 Post Office Avenue, Baltimore, Md., represented at Harrisburg, Pa., by JAMES LYNAIL

All true collieries that mine the true Franklin Coal of Lykens Valley, are managed by me, also under my management are the CAMERON, the LUKE FIDDLER, (or Burnside), the HICKORY SWAMP and the HICKORY RIDGE collieries of Shamokin. The product of these last four collieries will henceforth be known as the CAMERON COAL and will be as handsome a coal as can be sent to market.

Dealers wishing to procure both or either of the above coals, are cautioned that they must and can be obtained through no one else than the above named agents.

W. B. FOWLE, General Manager

WIESTLING'S PATENT COMBINATION DUMP CART.

Is the best, most convenient and cheapest mode of delivering coal. Every dealer should adopt it. Ordinary carts can easily be changed to dump two ways. Wagons with horizontal beds can be made to dump. Coal can be delivered across pavements into coal holes or cellars without soiling the pavement. For circulars or information, apply to—

GEO. B. WIESTLING,
Mont Alto, Franklin County, Pa.

THE HUDSON COAL CO.,

SHIPPERS OF

ANTHRACITE AND BITUMINOUS COALS,

GENERAL OFFICE, 17 NEWARK STREET, HOBOKEN, N. J.

Steamboats and Tugs may be coaled with despatch at any hour day or night, at our coal wharf, foot of Sixth St., Hoboken, N. J.

UPPER LEHIGH AND COUNCIL RIDGE,
Lehigh Red Ash Coals.
SUPERIOR IN QUALITY AND PREPARATION.

ADDRESS;

Whitney, McCreary & Kemmerer,

OFFICES:

137 South Second Street, Philadelphia.

Room 8, Trinity Building, New York.

Mansion House, Mauch Chunk.

JOHN WHITE, Agent at NEW YORK.

CAMPBELL TUCKER.   ALFRED TUCKER.

CAMPBELL TUCKER & Co.,

MINERS AND SHIPPERS OF

ANTHRACITE AND BITUMINOUS
COAL.

Best varieties of Coals and Cokes, for iron, railroad, general manufacturing and domestic uses.

OFFICE, 208 WALNUT ST., PHILADELPHIA.

SHAW BROS.,
MINERS AND SHIPPERS OF
George's Creek Cumberland.

GENERAL AGENTS OF

ATLANTIC and GEORGE'S CREEK, BLÆN AVON, CUMBERLAND and ELK LICK COAL CO.'S. WHARVES AT LOCUST POINT, BALTIMORE, GEORGETOWN, D. C., and ALEXANDRIA, VA.

WEST VIRGINIA
AND
YOUGHIOGHENY GAS COALS.

Office, 24 SECOND STREET,
Baltimore, Md.

Boston Office, 82 WATER STREET,
WARE B. GAY, Agent.

LEHIGH VALLEY COAL COMPANY,

MINERS AND SHIPPERS OF

LEHIGH,

WYOMING WHITE AND RED ASH,

(BALTIMORE VEIN.)

Office, Corner Courtlandt and Church Streets.
[COAL AND IRON EXCHANGE BUILDING.]
GEO. B. NEWTON, AGENT.

SHIPMENTS BY RAILROAD AND MORRIS CANAL DIRECT FROM THE MINES, AND FROM PERTH AMBOY AND JERSEY CITY FOR ALL POINTS.

FREDERIC A. POTTS,
WHOLESALE COAL AND IRON MERCHANT,

OLD COMPANY LEHIGH FROM SUMMIT HILL MINES.
HONEY BROOK SUPERIOR WHITE ASH LEHIGH. FULTON LEHIGH.
PLYMOUTH WYOMING—RED ASH.
WILKESBARRE COAL (BALTIMORE VEIN.)
DELAWARE, LACKAWANNA AND WESTERN CO'S SCRANTON.
PHILADELPHIA AND READING COAL AND IRON COMPANY'S SCHUYLKILL COAL.
GEORGE'S CREEK CUMBERLAND COAL—FROM THE WELL-KNOWN HAMPSHIRE MINE.

110 Broadway, [Metropolitan Bank Building,] - - - - - New York.
No. 33 Westminster Street, - - - - - - - - - - Providence, R. I.

NEWBURGH ORREL COAL CO.,

MINERS AND SHIPPERS OF

NEWBURGH ORREL, TYRCONNELL AND PALATINE

GAS COALS,

Mines situated at Newburgh, Flemington, and Fairmont, West Virginia.
C. OLIVER O'DONNELL, President.   CHAS. MACKALL, Secretary,
Home Office, 52 South Gay Street,   - - - Baltimore, Md.
Chas. W. Hays, Agent in New York, No. 111 Broadway, (Trinity Building.)
SHIPPING WHARVES AT LOCUST POINT.
References furnished when required, and special attention given to chartering of vessels.

MARYLAND COAL CO.,

MINERS AND SHIPPERS OF GEORGE'S CREEK

CUMBERLAND COAL,

OF THE BEST QUALITY,

Shipments from Baltimore or over improved railway schute from Georgetown in superior order.

OFFICES, 15 & 17 TRINITY BUILDING,
111 Broadway, NEW YORK.

ROBINSON, HAYDON & CO.,

SHIPPERS OF

"SPRING MOUNTAIN" LEHIGH,

AND WILKESBARRE COAL,

SHIPMENTS MADE TO ALL POINTS ACCESSIBLE FROM N. Y

OFFICE, ROOM 33 TRINITY BUILDING,
111 BROADWAY, N. Y.

OLIVER'S PATENT WATER-PROOF
DOUBLE-CAPPED CARTRIDGE,

This cartridge is intended for general use in the mines in place of the ordinary cartridge now made by the miner. The double-capped metal end not only forms a water-tight joint, but also acts as a shield to prevent the cartridge from being caught at the end by any sharp projections of coal. It is a perfectly water-proof cartridge. For sale to operators in quantities at moderate rates. Address,

PAUL A. OLIVER,
WILKESBARRE, PA

Walter, Donaldson & Co.,
SOLE AGENTS FOR THE SALE OF THE FOLLOWING

COAL:

"THOMAS LEHIGH," AND GIRARD MAMMOTH,
Shipped from Port Richmond, and via Schuylkill Canal.

WYOMING AND WILKESBARRE,
Shipped from Elizabethport, and via Lehigh Canal.

111 BROADWAY, NEW YORK.   17 DOANE STREET, BOSTON.

205 WALNUT STREET, PHILADELPHIA.

G. B. LINDERMAN & CO.,

Sugar Loaf & Humboldt, Lehigh Coal,

OFFICE—50 TRINITY BUILDING,

111 BROADWAY, — — — — — — — NEW YORK.

STEEL AND IRON WIRE ROPES,

For Mines, Inclined Planes, Wire Rope Tramways, Transmission of Power, Suspension Bridges, Ship's Rigging, etc, made by

The Hazard Manufacturing Company, Wilkesbarre, Penna.

This company has the Largest and Most Perfect Rope-making Machinery in the World. Capable of making ropes of any size, from Sash Cord to ropes sixty tons weight, without a splice.

NONE BUT THE VERY BEST MATERIAL USED.

These ropes are used more generally than any other throughout the Coal Regions. Reference is made to the Lehigh and Wilkesbarre Coal Company, the Riverside Coal Company, and others.

For Prices, Instructions on the Use of Wire Ropes, and other Information, address

THE HAZARD MANUFACTURING COMPANY,
Wilkesbarre, Penn.

R. H. WILLIAMS,

ANTHRACITE AND BITUMINOUS COALS,

Sole Agent for the

"Black Mine," Red Ash Coal.

FORMERLY KNOWN AS THE SPOHN VEIN.

56 BROADWAY, NEW YORK.

ROOM No. 7.

Pea and Dust Coal a Specialty.

WM. KENDRICK & CO.,

MINERS AND SHIPPERS OF

"BEAVER RUN" BITUMINOUS COAL,

(FROM CLEARFIED COUNTY, PA.)

GENERAL OFFICE, 113 WALNUT STREET, PHILADELPHIA

SHIPPING PIERS { GREENWICH POINT, PHILADELPHIA. SOUTH AMBOY, N. J.

General Agent for New York and Eastern markets,
WM. D. MARVEL, 60 TRINITY BUILDING
111 BROADWAY, NEW YORK

WILLIAM D. MARVEL,
COAL AND IRON MERCHANT

[ROOM 60 TRINITY BUILDING]

No. 111 Broadway,

NEW YORK.

P.O. Box 5422   ESTABLISHED 1868.

Anthracite and Bituminous Coals,
American and Foreign Pig Iron,
Charcoal Blooms and Billets for Steel Work,
Rail Road Rails,
Importer of Spanish and African
Iron Ore for Bessemer Works

AMERICAN SHOVEL CO.,

For Sale at 43 Trinity Building, 111 Broadway.

Factory,—Birmingham, Connecticut.

MANUFACTURERS OF
LOWMAN'S PATENT CAST STEEL

SHOVELS, SPADES AND SCOOPS,
OF ALL DESCRIPTIONS

Without straps or rivets, of the best English and American Cast Steel. Every Shovel Warranted. The attention of Railroad and Mining Companies is invited to this very economical shovel.

———C———

SAMUEL BONNELL, JR., Prest. GEO. TUTHILL, Sect'y.
THOS. KECK, Vice-President. C. B. SHOEMAKER, TREAS.

BLACK DIAMOND COAL,

A SUPERIOR WHITE ASH, FREE-BURNING COAL,
WELL PREPARED AND OF HANDSOME FRACTURE.

I have resumed the mining of coal, and shall be pleased to receive your orders, for the current year, for such of the **BLACK DIAMOND (WYOMING) COAL**, as you may require. The colliery is situated at Kingston, opposite Wilkesbarre, Pa., in the Wyoming Valley. I shall endeavor to continue the pleasant and satisfactory relations which have heretofore characterised my connection with the trade.

SAMUEL BONNELL, JR.,
Rooms 43 and 45 Trinity Building, 111 Broadway.

OLIVER'S POWDER.

THIS POWDER RECOMMENDS ITSELF ON ACCOUNT OF

ITS SUPERIOR STRENGTH
AND
FREEDOM FROM SMOKE.

NOW IN USE IN THE COAL REGIONS OF PENNSYLVANIA.

DIRECT ORDERS TO PAUL A. OLIVER, WILKESBARRE, PA.

C. E. DETMOLD.   JAMES S. COX.

DETMOLD & COX,

Rooms 38, 40 & 42 Trinity Building,   NEW YORK.

SUPPLY

RAILROAD COMPANIES, STEAMSHIP COMPANIES, MANUFACTURERS, and the TRADE GENERALLY,

WITH THE BEST QUALITIES OF

ANTHRACITE AND BITUMINOUS COAL,

ESPECIALLY,

Lehigh, George's Creek Cumberland, and the Clearfield County Coal, of the Kittaning Coal Co., of Penna.

THE MIDDLE LEHIGH COAL CO.,

OF MAUCH CHUNK, PA.

MINERS OF

"DETMOLD LEHIGH COAL,"

The ne plus ultra for Manufacturing and Domestic purposes.

NO SLATE.   NO SULPHUR.   NO CLINKERS.

AGENTS AND SHIPPERS,

DETMOLD & COX, 111 Broadway, New York.

PETROLEUM GAS.

Works have been built for making Fixed and Smokeless Gas from Petroleum by the undersigned, for the following parties:

    SUNBURY, PA. GAS CO.,
    MAHANOY CITY, PA. GAS LIGHT CO.,
    SHENANDOAH GAS LIGHT CO.,
    PLYMOUTH, PA. GAS LIGHT CO.,
    SHAMOKIN, PA. GAS LIGHT CO.,
    PHILADELPHIA AND READING R. R. CO.,
    COL. W. R. MURPHY, TRENTON, N. J.,
    NORRISTOWN, PA. GAS CO.,
    ASHLAND, PA. GAS LIGHT CO.,
    BLOOMSBURG, PA. GAS LIGHT CO.,
    DEFIANCE, OHIO. GAS LIGHT CO.,
    GOSHEN, INDIANA. GAS LIGHT CO., and others.

These are the only Oil Gas Works that will use with equal facility all the various grades of Petroleum, and that have NEVER FAILED TO GIVE ENTIRE SATISFACTION. Large consumers of Coal Gas, and parties who are not supplied with Gas, should not fail to have one of these works.

J. D. PATTON,

Trevorton, Northumberland Co., Pa.

THE CLOVER HILL RAILROAD COMPANY OF VIRGINIA,
BITUMINOUS COAL,

FOR GAS, RAILROAD, STEAMSHIP AND GENERAL USES. SHIPMENT BY VESSEL TO ALL POINTS.

GEORGE G. SAMPSON, SALES AGENT,

[Post Office Box 90.]   69 WILLIAM STREET, NEW YORK.

HOWELL FISHER & CO.

SOLE MINERS AND SHIPPERS OF

FISHER'S GATE VEIN

RED ASH COAL

And Dealers in

OTHER FIRST CLASS

ANTHRACITE COAL,

OFFICE: Room 47,

COAL & IRON EXCHANGE,

Courtland & Church Sts.,

W. J. HARLAN, Agent,   -   NEW YORK.

MAYER, CARROLL & CO.,

Miners and Shippers of the Celebrated

George's Creek Cumberland Coal,

AND

WEST VIRGINIA GAS AND CANNEL COAL.

SHIPPING WHARF, LOCUST POINT.

OFFICE, 13 GERMAN ST., NEAR SOUTH,

BALTIMORE, MD.

Particular attention given to the chartering of vessels, and the receipt and shipment of coal on consignment, for which we have ample facilities at our Locust Point wharf.

G. L. BOYD,

Manufacturer of

ROUND AND SQUARE WIRE,

AND

WROUGHT IRON

COAL SCREENS,

OF ALL DESCRIPTIONS

Tamaqua,   -   *Pennsylvania.*

L. S. BOYER & CO.,

ANTHRACITE,

BITUMINOUS

AND GAS

COALS,

No. 228 DOCK STREET,

PHILADELPHIA.

Agents for

Monongahela Gas Coal Company,

AND

KEYSTONE CUMBERLAND COAL.

PORTER, BELL & CO.

Outside Connected Mine Locomotive.

EXCLUSIVE SPECIALTY. } LIGHT LOCOMOTIVES.

From 7x12, to 14x20 Cylinders, and 10,000 to 50,000 pounds loaded weight. For 24 Inches Gauge and upwards, Light Rail, Sharp Curves, Heavy Loads, and Grades up to 300 feet per mile.

NARROW GAUGE PASSENGER and FREIGHT ENGINES, Light or Heavy.
SPECIAL SERVICE TANK OR TENDER ENGINES, over 20 sizes and styles.
MINE ENGINES with 4 or 6 Drivers, and Outside or Inside Connections, Conforming to Entry, *doing the work of 10 to 40 mules at less than cost of operating 3 mules and 3 drivers. Saving in track and cars, and no cost for keeping when mine is shut down.*

PHOTOGRAPH and PRICE OF ENGINE to do SPECIFIED WORK furnished on APPLICATION.

OFFICE—5 Monongahela House. }
WORKS—A. V. R. R. 49 and 50 Sts. }   PITTSBURGH, PENNA.

THE WESTMORELAND COAL CO.

(Chartered 1854.)

Mines situated on the Pennsylvania and the Connellsville Railroads, in Westmoreland county, Pennsylvania.

POINTS OF SHIPMENTS:

PENNSYLVANIA RAILROAD PIER, No. 2 (upper side), GREENWICH, DELAWARE RIVER; PIER, No. 1 (upper side), SOUTH AMBOY, N. J.

Since the commencement of operations by this company its well-known

BITUMINOUS COAL

has been largely used by the Gas Companies, Railroads and Iron and Steel Works, in the New England and Middle States, and its character is established as having no superior for freedom from sulphur and other impurities.

Principal Office—No. 230 South Third Street, Philadelphia.

EDWARD C. BIDDLE,   FRANCIS H. JACKSON,   EDMUND H. McCULLOUGH,
President.   Vice-President.   Secretary.

W. H. PIPER,
Miner & Shipper of the Celebrated
"COALDALE" Bituminous Coal,
OFFICE, 314½ WALNUT STREET, PHILADELPHIA.

HUDDELL & SEITZINGER,
MINERS AND SHIPPERS OF COAL.

Sole Agents for the Sale of the following celebrated Coals,

HARLEIGH LEHIGH COAL, HICKORY AND DRAPER COALS,
EXCELSIOR COAL MINING COMPANY'S SHAMOKIN COAL
AND THE
"LORBERRY COAL," FROM WEST END AND COLKET COLLIERIES.

OFFICES:
207 WALNUT STREET, PHILADELPHIA; 111 BROADWAY, NEW YORK;
13 KILBY STREET, BOSTON.

S. H. BROWN & CO.,
WHOLESALE COAL MERCHANTS,

No. 19 Exchange Place, Boston; Coal and Iron Exchange Building,
New York; First National Bank Building, Wilkes-Barre, Pa.

SOLE AGENTS FOR THE CELEBRATED

NORTH FRANKLIN Red and White Ash and SUSQUEHANNA COAL CO'S Red and White Ash Coals, also other SCHUYLKILL, LACKAWANNA and LEHIGH COALS.

Shipments made at SOUTH AMBOY, N. J. and DELAWARE CITY, Delaware.

A. Pardee, Hazleton, Pa.   J. G. Fell, Philadelphia

A. PARDEE & CO.,
303 WALNUT STREET, - - PHILADELPHIA.

MINERS AND SHIPPERS OF
LEHIGH COALS.

The following superior and well-known coals are mined by ourselves and firms connected with us, viz.
HAZLETON, SUGAR LOAF, CRANBERRY, JEDDO, HIGHLAND, LATTIMER.

OFFICES:
WM. LILLY, Mauch Chunk, Pa.,   WM. MENSHON, 111 Broadway, N. Y.
O. D. WITHERELL, 05 State Street, Boston, Mass.

BLÆN AVON COAL CO.,
OF ALLEGHANY COUNTY, MD.

GEORGE'S CREEK
CUMBERLAND COAL.
Shipped at Georgetown, Alexandria and Baltimore.

ANDREW SPIER, President,   -   *CUMBERLAND, MD.*

General Sales Agents.

SHAW BROS.,   24 Second Street,   BALTMIMORE.

BRADFORD'S
Coal and Ore Separators,

For Separating Slate, Bone Coal, and other impurities from

Anthracite and Bituminous Coal,

And also all impurities from Iron, Lead, Silver, Gold, and other Ores,

For Sale by

H. BRADFORD, 26 Merchants' Exchange,

Corner Third and Walnut Streets,   PHILADELPHIA.

Baldwin Locomotive Works.

MINE LOCOMOTIVES.

Inside and outside connected. Adapted to rails of 16 lbs. per yard and upward. Will do the work of 30 to 40 mules on long hauls. Cost of operating not over $5.00 per day.

FREE PARTICULARS FURNISHED ON APPLICATION.

BURNHAM, PARRY, WILLIAMS & CO. Philadelphia.

RIEHLE BROTHERS,
Philadelphia Scale and Testing Machine Works,
NINTH ST., ABOVE MASTER, PHILA.

Patented Coal, Hay, And Cattle Scales.

Patented Self-Adjusting Railroad Track Scales.

The Celebrated Furnace Charging Scales.

Extra Heavy Rolling Mill Scales.

Warehouse and Dormant Scales.

Hopper Scales.

Portable platform Scales.

Testing Machines, for ascertaining the Strength of Iron Metals, Girders, Chains, &c.

www.ingramcontent.com/pod-product-compliance
Lightning Source LLC
Chambersburg PA
CBHW031409160426
43196CB00007B/955